# The All-Color

# CAKE DECORATING COURSE

# The All-Color

# CAKE DECORATING COURSE

A step-by-step guide to making traditional and fantasy cakes

## Elaine MacGregor

**HPBooks**®

**ANOTHER BEST-SELLING VOLUME FROM HP BOOKS**®

Published by HP Books®, P.O. Box 5367, Tuscon, A2 85703
ISBN: Hardcover 0-89586-474-6
Library of Congress Catalog Card Number: 86-81048

This book was designed and produced by
Quarto Publishing Ltd
The Old Brewery, 6 Blundell Street
London N7 9BH

**Senior Editors** Jan Thiesen (HP), Jane Rollason
**Editors** Linda Sonntag, Barbara Croxford, Lorraine Johnston

**Art Editor** Moira Clinch
**Design** Anthony Bussey, Penny Dawes, Rita Wütrich
**Photographers** David Burch, Zul Mukhida
**Illustrator** Mick Hill
**Paste-up Artist** Patrizio Semproni

**Publisher** Rick Bailey (HP)
**Art Director** Alastair Campbell
**Executive Editor** Randy Summerlin (HP)
**Editorial Directors** Elaine Woodard (HP), Jim Miles

Typeset by Ampersand Typesetting Ltd
Manufactured in Hong Kong by Regent Publishing Services Limited
Printed by Leefung-Asco Printers Ltd, Hong Kong

# CONTENTS

# PREFACE

*It is a popular fallacy that cooks are born and not made and, because of this, many people lack the confidence to attempt all but the simplest home baking. In fact most people can succeed with more adventurous projects if they are simply shown what to do. You may surprise yourself, your family and your friends. The aim of 'The All-Color Cake Decorating Course' is to help you learn and refine the skills of cake decorating and use them to create spectacular cakes.*

*Interest in cake decorating has grown dramatically in recent years. Throughout the world there are enthusiastic societies of cake decorators who meet regularly to exchange ideas, learn new techniques and hold exhibitions and competitions. This book is intended for experienced cake decorators as well as beginners and I hope there are new ideas in it for everybody.*

*Many of the techniques demonstrated in this book will appeal to those whose time is limited, because they provide new and quick methods of preparing a cake for its final decoration. This applies in particular to Australian fondant icing or sugar paste and buttercream.*

*I have tried to take away from cake decorating some of the mysteries of 'sugar art' by showing how to achieve different effects in step-by-step sequences. Like most other skills, the techniques of cake decorating are quite easy to understand and perform if they are broken down into a logical sequence of simple steps.*

*Do not hurry or panic and do not worry if your first attempts are not successful. If, for example, you are making a delicate collar, sugar lace or a sugar flower for a celebration cake, then you are working with skills which even professional confectioners and bakers do not regularly practice. In our cost-sensitive world producing such time-consuming and elaborate work is not commercially viable. And even the experts occasionally have off-days, when they feel as if their hands are encased in boxing gloves.*

*In the second half of the book you will find both simple and elaborate cakes, although it is not always possible to identify which is which at first glance. They are all elegant and the skills involved in making them are covered in the first half of the course. These lessons are the product of many years of practicing and teaching the art of cake decorating. It is essential to be thoroughly familiar with the techniques involved before attempting an elaborate cake.*

*You do not have to follow the designs and patterns slavishly, although you may prefer to do so to begin with. Do not be put off by the photographs of the finished cakes – they are meant to be perfect in order to show you what to aim at. Mistakes can be hidden with all kinds of decoration or simply turned to the back where they cannot be seen. Stand back and accept the compliments of friends and family on your edible work of art. The comment, 'it looks too good to eat', however, should not be taken too literally in this case.*

*I would like to thank everyone who has assisted in the preparation of this book and in particular Linda Sonntag for preparing the text from notes and all my friends at Woodnutt's.*

*Elaine MacGregor*

*ABOVE:* The author, Elaine MacGregor (center right) is pictured with her husband Stuart MacGregor (center left) and Woodnutt's teaching staff, Pauline Giles and Alex Bransgrove.

*LEFT:* Max Schofield (left) and Greg Robinson of Crumbs of London designed and made most of the fantasy cakes contained in Section Two of the book.

# SECTION ONE

# CAKE MAKING

Successful cake decorating relies on successful cake making. There is no point in spending hours elaborately decorating a cake that has not been properly baked. By following a few simple rules and using a good recipe, you can ensure a good result every time. It is particularly important to know your oven and make any minor adjustments to baking times and temperatures that are necessary.

Eight recipes are given in this section for traditional sponge cake and fruit cake mixes, and these are the cakes used for decoration in Section 2 of the course. You may have your own tried and tested recipes and you can, of course, use these instead.

This section also gives advice on equipment, preparing cake pans, cooling, storing and freezing cakes, and how to test whether your cake is cooked and avoid common baking mistakes.

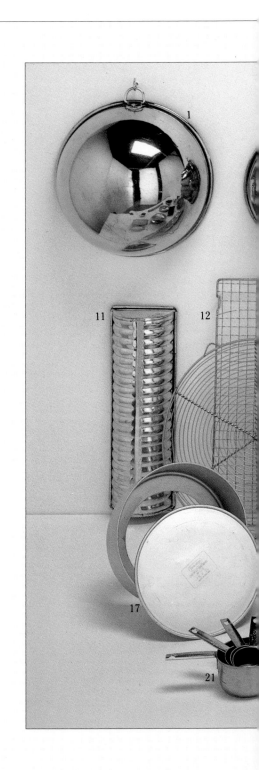

A few basic rules apply to baking, which when observed remove many of the uncertainties and help avoid possible mistakes.

Clean and dry all the equipment required. Grease and line the baking pans. Use the right utensils for weighing, testing, sifting, grinding, grating and chopping.

Before baking, switch on the oven to pre-heat it to the correct temperature. The oven should be well-insulated and draft-proof, as a discrepancy of a few degrees in the temperature can have a disastrous effect.

A comprehensive selection of baking equipment is illustrated above.

1  Copper egg white bowl
2  Gugelhupf mold
3  Measuring spoon
4  Plastic spatula or scraper
5  Nylon mesh sieve
6  Metal spatula
7  Large metal spoon for folding in
8  Large cake server or spatula
9  Balloon whisk
10 Candy thermometer
11 Guttered mold or Rehrücken pan
12 Wire cooling racks
13 Deep cupcake or muffin pans
14 Jelly roll pan

15 Angel cake pan
16 Madeleine pans
17 Deep, loose-bottomed cake pan
18 Fluted pie plates with loose bottoms
19 Loaf pans
20 Spring-form pans
21 Measuring cups
22 Patterned ring or savarin mold
23 Unlined copper sugar boiler
24 Cookie cutters
25 Plain rolling pin
26 Pastry brush

# PREPARING CAKE PANS

To get the best results from decorating a fruit cake, whether you are planning to cover it with royal icing, fondant icing or glacé icing, it is essential to work on a cake with a good smooth finish. This is why correctly lining the cake pan, to give the cake a firm even shape, is of such vital importance. A light sponge cake will need little or no lining, while a fruit cake, particularly if it is to have a long baking time, needs proper insulation.

## LINING PAPER

You can use either wax or parchment paper to line the pan. Pack the cake well in order to get a good finish.

Whatever shape cake pan you use, be it round, oval, heart-shaped, square, hexagonal or octagonal, you will need only two simple techniques for shaping the paper to line curves or angles.

## CAKE HATS

Although oven temperatures can be perfectly regulated, it may be a good idea to cut a 'hat' for the cake to prevent it from drying on top. This is a double thickness of paper approximately 2 inches bigger than the cake pan. It should rest, not on the cake batter, but on the 1 inch of paper that rises above the sides of the pan. Put it on as soon as the cake goes into the oven. This is a pointless exercise if your oven is a fan or convection model, because it will be blown off.

## LINING A ROUND PAN

**1** To line a round pan with wax paper, place the pan base down on the wax paper and draw a circle around it. Cut the circle out about ¼ inch inside the line to allow for the thickness of the pan. Cut out another circle, the same size, for the base because you will need a double thickness for better insulation.

**2** To line the sides of the pan, put the pan on its side on the paper. Make a pencil mark where the pan touches the paper, roll the pan along until you reach the same point and make another mark. Use the joint in the pan as a starting point if there is one. Add 2 inches for overlap. Cut the strip 2 inches wider than the depth of the pan, so that you have 1 inch to turn in at the base and the same amount overlapping the top of the pan. You need a double thickness, so cut two linings for the sides.

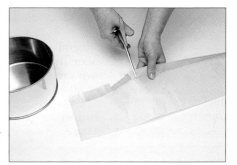

**3** To make the side lining fit the base of the pan, fold it to a depth of 1 inch along its length. With any curved pan, snip the paper along its length, at intervals of ¼ inch, to the depth of the fold.

**4** Now slip the lining into the pan. The nicks will overlap and the paper will fit the curve of the pan snugly. When you have lined the sides of the pan with two layers of wax paper, drop in the two base liners. You should have a perfect fit. Brush the wax paper with clarified butter, vegetable shortening or margarine to coat it evenly. Non-stick parchment paper does not need greasing.

## LINING A SQUARE PAN OR CAKE FRAME

**1** To line a square pan or cake frame with wax or parchment paper, first place the pan on the paper and mark out the base. With a cake frame, draw inside the base. With a pan, draw around it.

**2** Cut out the square, remembering to make it ¼ inch smaller than your outline if you have drawn around the outside of a cake pan, to allow for the thickness of the pan. Cut another square the same size. You will need a double thickness for the base.

**3** To line the sides of the pan or frame, put it on its side on the paper. Make a pencil mark where the pan touches the paper, roll the pan along until you reach the same point and make another mark. Add on 2 inches for overlap. Then cut a strip 2 inches wider than the depth of the pan, so that you have 1 inch to turn in at the base and the same amount overlapping the top.

**4** To make the side lining fit the base of the pan or frame, fold it to a depth of 1 inch along its length, starting about half way along one side of the pan

so that the paper joint does not end up in a corner. Use a distinguishing mark on the pan, such as a joint, or mark the pan so that you know where you started. Now turn the pan along the paper again, and mark each angle with a pencil, remembering that you are lining the inside of the pan and not the outside and allowing for the width of the pan. It is much safer to mark the paper in this way, rather than dividing your paper into four for a square or eight for an octagon, because very often pans are not exactly true to shape.

**5** When you have marked all the angles of the pan, fold the paper along the pencil marks. Make a good firm crease for each angle and check that you are keeping the base parallel, so that the creases run up-

wards from it at a 90° angle. Now snip along the creases at ¼ inch intervals from the edge of the paper to the depth of your 1 inch fold.

**6** Fold out the paper to the shape of the pan and you will see that you have very neat, right-angled corners to fit its shape. With a straight-sided pan, be it square, hexagonal or octagonal, you only have to nick the folded edges at the corners and not all the way along, as with a curved edge, to get a good fit. Slide the side lining into the pan, or into the cake frame on a baking sheet, to fit it snugly. Put in the two layers of base lining.

*The cooked cake BELOW comes out of the oven with beautifully squared corners.*

## LINING A JELLY ROLL PAN

**1** To line a jelly roll pan, place the pan on wax paper and draw around the base. Increase the rectangle by 2 inches at each side to allow for the depth of the pan plus overlap. Cut out the rectangle and nick each of the corners diagonally down to the size of the original rectangle, subtracting ¼ inch for the thickness of the pan.

**2** Fold the rectangle to fit the base of the pan. As you put the paper into the pan, the nicked edges will overlap to form right-angled corners. Secure the corners in position with staples or paperclips.

**3** Brush the lining with clarified butter, vegetable shortening oil or margarine and dust it with flour.

*Draw round the base of your pan and cut out the circle just inside the line, allowing for the thickness of the pan.*

## BAKING SPONGE CAKES

There is no need to line the pan if you are baking a light cake, such as a Victoria sponge cake or a Genoese or Whisked sponge cake, though some people do like to put a layer of paper in the base of the pan. All you need to do is brush the pan with clarified butter, vegetable shortening or margarine and then dust it with flour and sugar. Always use a brush rather than your fingers to grease the pan to ensure an even coat.

# COOLING, STORING & FREEZING

## COOLING

When you turn your cake out of the pan, do not turn it on to a wire rack. The lattice pattern of the rack will be imprinted on it as the cake settles. To get a clean finish you would then have to fill in the imprints before putting on the marzipan.

**1** Let fruit cake cool completely in the pan. You will then find that you can lift it out of the pan quite easily by pulling the paper jutting above the sides of the pan.

**2** Turn a sponge cake out on to a sheet of wax paper dusted with superfine sugar. The sugar will give a good finish when you turn the cake over.

**3** When you peel the paper from the cooled cake it will come away cleanly, leaving the cake with perfectly smooth sides. If the paper has stuck to the cake, brush the paper with cold water and it will peel away more easily.

## STORING

Rich fruit cakes were originally made as a means of preserving summer fruit for the winter months. They would then be stored for long periods. Today, though the fruits they are made with are available all year round, there is still good reason for keeping a cake for two or three months before you decorate it. The taste of the individual ingredients becomes less distinct as the cake ages and their flavors mingle into richness.

**1** To store the cake before you marzipan it, leave it in the paper you baked it in to protect it against getting knocked and having its shape spoiled.

**2** The best way of keeping a cake for two or three months before marzipanning it is to wrap it first in one or two layers of wax paper. Then wrap it in a tea towel or aluminium foil. Do not store it in a pan or wrap it directly in plastic wrap or aluminium foil. Unless you vacuum pack a cake inside a pan, you will be sealing stale air in with the cake. If you wrap it in plastic wrap, it will sweat. If you wrap it in foil, the natural acids in the fruit will eat through the aluminium and when you come to decorate the cake you will find the foil full of little holes.

**3** While the cake is aging, you can sprinkle it periodically with brandy or rum or any spirit of your choice. You can make holes in the cake with a skewer, then pour on a tablespoon of alcohol. Alternatively you can buy a syringe from a drug store and inject the cake to avoid it being full of large holes. Sprinkling a cake periodically definitely improves its flavor. Be careful not to add too much alcohol, however, or it will become wet and difficult to handle.

## FREEZING & DEFROSTING

Sponge cakes and soft-iced cakes freeze well and can be stored over a period of months. Fruit cakes and hard-iced cakes can also be frozen, but they are better stored in a cool, dry atmosphere.

### FREEZING

**Sponge cakes**
Uncooked cake batter can be stored for up to 6 weeks in an airtight container in the freezer. A baked sponge cake should be frozen as soon as it has cooled. Wrap it in freezer wrap and freeze it for up to 4 months.

**Fruit cakes**
A fruit cake can be frozen in the same way as a sponge cake. It is not necessary to freeze a fruit cake, however, and the freezing process actually inhibits the development of the flavor in the cake.

**Soft-iced cakes**
Cakes coated with a soft icing, such as buttercream or whipped cream, are particularly suitable for freezing. They must be tightly wrapped in freezer wrap, as cream-based mixtures tend to absorb flavors from foodstuffs around them if exposed to the air.
During defrosting, the cake will attract condensation and any food colors may run a little. When you take the cake from its wrappings, do not attempt to wipe away any condensation from the surface of the cake. Allow it to dry naturally.

### DEFROSTING

**Soft-iced cakes**
The packaging should be removed before defrosting. Allow 6 to 12 hours for the cake to defrost.

**Hard-iced cakes**
It is essential to leave a royal or fondant iced cake in its wrapping for 24 to 48 hours, depending on its size, while it defrosts.
During defrosting, the cake will attract condensation and any food colors may run a little. When unwrapped, do not attempt to wipe away any condensation from the surface of the cake. Allow it to dry naturally.

# VICTORIA SPONGE CAKE

Recipes for sponge cake go back a good 300 years and it remains one of today's favorites.

The basic ingredients for a Victoria Sponge Cake are equal quantities of butter, sugar, flour and eggs. All of the ingredients must be room temperature before you start or the cake will not rise properly. If your kitchen is cold, it is a good idea to warm the ingredients over a bowl of hot water; never put them in the oven or they will start to cook.

You can either use self-rising or all-purpose flour with a leavening agent in it. It should be sifted at least once, and preferably twice, after measuring.

If you have difficulty locating superfine sugar, process granulated sugar in the blender or food processor to reduce the size of the crystals.

### INGREDIENTS
1½ cups unsalted butter, room temperature
1½ cups superfine sugar
3 cups (7 oz.) self rising flour, sifted or
   3 cups (7 oz.) all-purpose flour and
   1 tablespoon baking powder, sifted
6 large eggs, room temperature
jam or buttercream

**1** Preheat the oven to 350°F. Prepare two 8×2-inch layer pans and put them aside.

**2** Using a large bowl, beat the butter for at least 1 minute or until light and fluffy.

**3** Gradually add the sugar and beat until the mixture is pale yellow, soft and very light, scraping the bowl often.

**4** Add the eggs one at a time. It is a good idea to break each egg into a small bowl or cup and beat it lightly with a fork before adding it to the creamed mixture. Beat well after each addition. Do not add the eggs too quickly or the batter will appear curdled. If the batter starts to separate, add a spoonful of the flour and beat thoroughly.

**5** Add the flour 1 cup at a time, folding with a rubber spatula. Work quickly but gently; do not beat.

**6** Divide the batter between the prepared pans. Bake for 25 to 30 minutes or until the cakes are golden brown. The cake should feel firm but springy when lightly touched with the finger. If the cake is not quite cooked, your finger will leave an impression in it. Let the cake cool in the pan for a few minutes before turning on to a rack to cool completely.

Finish the cake in the traditional manner by sandwiching the two halves together with jam or buttercream.

### VARIATIONS
The Victoria Sponge Cake is very versatile because it can be flavored in so many different ways.
Chocolate: Add 4 ounces melted, cooled, semisweet chocolate to the creamed butter or sift ½ cup unsweetened cocoa with the flour.
Orange: Finely grate the zest of 2 oranges and add it to the creamed mixture along with ¼ cup orange juice before folding in the flour.
Lemon: Finely grate the zest of 2 lemons and add it to the creamed mixture along with 2 tablespoons lemon juice before folding in the flour.
Coffee: Dissolve 1 tablespoon instant coffee in 1 teaspoon hot water and let it cool before adding to the creamed mixture.
Almond: Add ½ teaspoon almond extract to the creamed mixture and ⅔ cup finely ground almonds to the sifted flour. Use 2½ cups flour instead of 3 cups.

# ONE-STAGE SPONGE CAKE

For the One-Stage Sponge Cake, use the same ingredients in almost the same proportions as for the Victoria Sponge Cake. Again, these ingredients must be at room temperature.

This method is quick and easy but, since the ingredients are not added gradually, there will not be as much air in the batter to make it rise as well as the Victoria. For this reason you will need to use self-rising flour and baking powder. Do not be tempted to add more baking powder because you will be able to taste it and it will not make the cake rise further.

Do not overbeat the batter in an attempt to make it lighter; the cake will, instead, be tough.

### INGREDIENTS
2¼ cups (9¾ oz.) self-rising flour, sifted
1 teaspoon baking powder
1 cup (8 oz.) unsalted butter, room temperature
1 cup superfine sugar
4 large eggs, room temperature

1 Preheat the oven to 350°F. Prepare two 8×2-inch layer pans and set them aside.

2 Sift the flour and baking powder together. Combine all ingredients in a large bowl. Beat for about 1 minute with an electric mixer or for about 2 minutes using a wooden spoon, until ingredients are well blended.

3 Divide the batter between the prepared pans, smoothing the tops. Bake 25 to 30 minutes. (See Victoria Sponge Cake, Step 6, for doneness test.) Let the cake cool in the pan for a few minutes before turning on to a rack to cool completely.

# GENOESE CAKE

The Genoese is a fine-textured, moist cake, ideal for cutting and making small petits fours and gateaux. Its moistness is due to the high proportion of butter and eggs to flour.

### INGREDIENTS
7 tbsp unsalted butter, room temperature
½ cup plus 1 tablespoon superfine sugar
4 large eggs, room temperature
¾ cup plus 2 tbsp self-rising flour, sifted or
   ¾ cup plus 2 tbsp all purpose flour with
   1 tsp baking powder, sifted

1 Preheat the oven to 350°F. Prepare one 8-inch springform pan or two 8×2-inch layer pans; set aside.

2 Melt the butter in a small bowl over a saucepan of hot water. Allow it to cool slightly; it must not be hot when it is added to the batter.

3 Using an electric mixer, beat the sugar and eggs together at high speed until the mixture has doubled in volume, 10 to 15 minutes. When properly beaten, the mixture should drop in a slowly dissolving ribbon when the beaters are lifted.

4 Sift one-fourth of the flour over the mixture and fold it in using a rubber spatula. Pour about one-third of the butter over the batter and fold it in quickly but gently. Working quickly, continue alternating flour and butter and fold just until batter is well combined.

5 Pour the batter into the prepared pan(s). Bake layer cakes 18 to 20 minutes and springform about 30 to 35 minutes, or until cake shrinks slightly from sides of pan. Let cool in pan a few minutes before turning on to rack to cool completely.

# WHISKED SPONGE CAKE

This classic sponge cake is made without butter and keeps fresh for quite a few days. Although you use all purpose flour there is no need for baking powder; what makes the cake rise so well is the increased beating, which incorporates air into the batter. Baking powder is often useful for making a cake rise, but it does have the disadvantage of drying it out. A whipped sponge cake stays moist and keeps well.

The flour and eggs should be at room temperature. Warm them slightly in a bowl over a larger bowl of warm water if your kitchen is cool. Make sure that your oven is preheated and your cake pans prepared before you begin. Once the batter is in the pans it should go into the oven immediately.

### INGREDIENTS
6 large eggs, room temperature
¾ cup superfine sugar
1½ cups (6½ oz.) all-purpose flour, sifted

1 Preheat the oven to 350°F. Grease and flour one 8×3-inch springform pan or two 8×2-inch layer pans; set aside.

2 Combine the eggs and sugar in the large bowl of the electric mixer. Beat on high speed 10 to 15 minutes, until the mixture is pale, thick and creamy and twice its original volume. When it is properly beaten, the mixture should fall from the beaters in a ribbon.

3 Sift the flour ½ cup at a time over the surface. Using a rubber spatula, quickly and carefully fold in flour until it is completely incorporated. The batter should have the consistency of lightly whipped cream. If it is too thick, add a few drops of warm water.

4 Pour the batter into the prepared pan(s). Bake springform about 40 minutes and layer pans 20 to 25 minutes. (See Victoria Sponge Cake, Step 6, for doneness test.) Let cake cool in the pan for a few minutes before turning on to a rack to cool completely.

This recipe may also be used for a simple jolly roll.

19

# JELLY ROLL

You can make a jelly roll with the Whipped Sponge Cake batter or you can use the recipe below. Make sure that your pan is lined, greased and dusted with superfine sugar, that your oven is preheated and that all your ingredients are room temperature or gently warmed before you begin.

### INGREDIENTS
¾ cup plus 2 tbsp sifted all-purpose flour
1 tbsp cornstarch
1½ tsp baking powder
4 large egg whites, room temperature
a pinch of salt
1 cup superfine sugar
4 large egg yolks, room temperature
1 tbsp cold water
1 tsp lemon juice or orange-flavored extract
jam
whipped cream or buttercream, if desired

**1** Preheat the oven to 350°F. Prepare a 15½×10½×1-inch jelly roll pan by lining it with wax paper, oiling lightly and dusting with a little superfine sugar; put aside.

**2** Sift the flour, cornstarch and baking powder together. In a large bowl beat the egg whites and salt with electric mixer until soft peaks form. Beat in 4 tablespoons sugar 1 tablespoon at a time and beat until stiff peaks form.

**3** In another large bowl beat the egg yolks until thick and lemon-colored. Gradually add the water, lemon juice or orange extract and all but 1 tablespoon of the sugar and beat until the mixture falls from the beaters in an unbroken, pale yellow ribbon.

**4** Gently stir about ¼ of the whites into the yolks to loosen the mixture, then fold in the remaining whites. Fold in the flour, being careful to retain as much volume as possible.

**5** Pour the batter into the prepared pan, spreading it evenly. Tap the pan lightly on the counter to remove any air bubbles. Bake 12 to 15 minutes, until cake tests done.

**6** Sprinkle a sheet of wax or parchment paper liberally with superfine sugar. To help prevent the cake from breaking or cracking when removing it from the pan, it is a good idea to lay the paper on top of a dish cloth that has been wrung out in hot water.

**7** When the cake is done, turn the pan upside down onto the sugar-sprinkled paper. Remove the lining paper as quickly as possible – if it sticks, dampen it slightly. Cut off any crisp cake edges with a sharp knife. Spread the cake fairly generously with warmed jam. Starting from short side,

# MADEIRA CAKE

roll cake tightly for the first turn and then more loosely.

**8** If you want to fill the jelly roll with whipped cream or buttercream, roll it up with the paper inside and let it stand until completely cold. Unroll the cake gently; remove and discard the paper. Spread the cake with filling and roll it back up again. (You often get a better-looking cake if you use jam only since just one rolling is necessary.)

Madeira Cake can be used for all the cakes which involve a lot of cutting and shaping before the marzipan and icing are added. In order to achieve good angles and curves the cake should be compact in texture and able to withstand pressure while remaining moist and flavorful.

### INGREDIENTS
¾ cup unsalted butter, room temperature
¾ cup superfine sugar
3 large eggs, room temperature
1½ cups sifted self-rising flour
½ cup sifted all-purpose flour
1 tbsp lemon juice
2 tsp lemon zest
2 tsp vanilla

**1** Preheat the oven to 350°F. Preheat an 8-inch springform or 8-inch square pan; set aside.

**2** Using an electric mixer cream the butter and the sugar until mixture is light and fluffy. Add the eggs one at a time (see Victoria Sponge Cake, page 16, Step 4), followed by a spoonful of the self-rising flour, and beat thoroughly.

**3** Sift the remaining flours together. Fold gently into the batter using a rubber spatula. Try to retain as much volume as possible. Fold in the lemon juice, lemon zest and vanilla.

**4** Turn the mixture into the prepared pan(s), smoothing the top. Bake about 45 to 50 minutes, until cake shrinks slightly from sides of pan. Let the cake cool in the pan for 5 to 10 minutes. Sprinkle wax or parchment paper liberally with sugar. Turn the cake out on to the paper, remove the lining paper and let cake cool completely.

# LIGHT FRUIT CAKE

A fruitcake is not as light as a sponge cake so it does not need to be beaten as much. The dried fruit soaks up the liquor or orange juice and is plumped out during baking. The result is a very moist cake.

### INGREDIENTS

1½ cups (8 oz.) dried mixed fruit, chopped
¼ cup brandy, sherry or orange juice
1 cup (8 oz.) unsalted butter, room temperature
1 cup superfine sugar
4 large eggs, room temperature
2 cups all-purpose flour, sifted

1 Combine fruit and liquor or orange juice in small bowl and let soak until liquid is absorbed, at least 2 hours.

2 Preheat the oven to 325°F. Prepare an 8-inch springform pan by lining bottom and sides with wax paper; set aside.

3 Using an electric mixer cream the butter and sugar until light and fluffy. Lightly beat the eggs. Add a little at a time to the creamed mixture and beat well. (Do not worry if mixture appears curdled.)

4 Stir in the fruit mix. Using a rubber spatula, gently fold in the flour until completely incorporated.

5 Turn the batter into the pan, smoothing the top and then making a slight indentation in the center of the cake. Bake about 1¼ hours. Let the cake cool in the pan before turning it out onto a rack.

# RICH FRUIT CAKE

This recipe uses equal amounts of fruits and nuts, plus butter, eggs, flour and sugar. Use the chart on the following page to find the exact quantities for the size cake you prefer.

### INGREDIENTS
1⅓ cups/8 oz golden raisins
1⅓ cups/8 oz dark raisins
1⅓ cups/8 oz currants
⅔ cup/4 oz halved candied cherries
⅓ cup/2 oz unblanched coarsely chopped almonds
⅓ cup/2 oz mixed candied peel (optional)
½ cup sherry or brandy, sherry and brandy mixed, or range juice, for soaking the fruit
2 cups all-purpose flour
½ cup self-rising flour
1 tsp mixed spices
1 tsp ground cinnamon
¼ tsp grated nutmeg
¼ tsp salt
½ cup/2 oz ground almonds
1 cup/8 oz. butter, room temperature
1⅓ cups/8 oz firmly packed dark brown sugar
4 eggs

1 In a medium bowl soak the raisins, currants, cherries, chopped almonds and peel overnight in the sherry and/or brandy, or orange juice.

2 Prepare pan(s) according to amounts listed in chart on page 24 and set aside. Position rack in center of oven and preheat oven to 425°F.

3 In another medium bowl sift together the two flours, mixed spices, cinnamon, nutmeg and salt. Stir in the ground almonds.

4 In a large bowl and using an electric mixer cream together the butter and sugar. Lightly beat the eggs in a small bowl. Add a little at a time to the creamed butter and mix well.

5 Alternately stir the flour and fruit mixtures into the butter in small amounts – do not beat the batter.

6 Turn the batter into the prepared pan(s). To fill evenly, hold the lining paper flat in the center of the pan with one hand and put a spoonful of batter in each of the four corners or edges. Add batter to fill the center. Then spoon in the remaining batter to come to within ¾-inch from top of pan. Smooth the top with a spoon, making sure that the fruit is covered by the batter so it will not dry out or burn during baking. Unless pan is loose-bottomed, lift it to a height of about 18 inches and drop it back onto the countertop to release air bubbles and allow mixture to settle.

7 Reduce oven heat to 275°F and bake cake(s) according to the time recommended on page 24.

# AMERICAN CHRISTMAS CAKE

A delux cake using whole fruit and nuts.

### INGREDIENTS
¾ cup pitted dates
½ cup candied pineapple
½ cup candied apricots
½ cup red candied cherries
½ cup green candied cherries
1 cup whole blanched almonds
1½ cups shelled brazil nuts
1 cup seeded raisins
⅔ cup golden raisins
2 eggs
½ cup brown sugar lightly packed
1 teaspoon vanilla extract
1 tablespoon rum, brandy, or sweet sherry
7 tablespoons butter
1 cup all-purpose flour
½ teaspoon baking powder
Pinch salt

**1** Preheat the oven to 270°F.

**2** Lightly grease an 8″ ring pan or mold or a 10″×4″ loaf pan. Chop the pineapple and apricots into fairly large pieces, and leave the remaining fruit and nuts whole. Mix all the fruit well together and reserve ½ cup combined nuts and candied fruit for garnishing.

**3** Beat the eggs until light and fluffy, then add the sugar, vanilla extract, rum and softened butter. Continue beating until well blended.

**4** Sift the flour with the baking powder and salt and add to the creamed batter with the fruit and nuts. Mix thoroughly.

**5** Spoon the mixture into the prepared pan and arrange the reserved fruit and nuts over the top, pressing down gently. Bake for about 1½ hours, or until the cake is firm to the touch. Let cool for 10 minutes in the pan before turning out.

---

## BAKING FRUIT CAKES

The information in this chart is based on the recipe for rich fruit cake given on page 23. The quantities given in the recipe are sufficient for a 3-inch deep, 8-inch round or 7-inch square cake. Find the size of cake you are making in the chart and increase or decrease the quantities of ingredients as shown in the second column.

The recipe for rich fruit cake works extremely well if followed exactly, but slight variation in the quantities of the fruit ingredients will not make much difference. Mixed peel can be left out, for example, or more cherries could be added to taste. The ratio of eggs: butter:flour, however, should be followed exactly.

If you want to use an irregular-shaped pan, such as a heart, hexagon or petal, you can assess the amount of mixture you will need by filling the pan with water. Transfer the water to a regular-shaped pan, round or square, which you have used to bake a fruit batter in before and judge what proportion of water you need to add or pour out to equal the amount of mixture the regular pan would normally hold. Increase or decrease the quantities of cake batter accordingly.

The long, slow baking advised in the chart results in a very dark cake which is not burnt at the edges. If you do not get satisfactory results, refer to the page opposite on testing cakes.

Once the cake has cooled, you can spike it with a skewer and pour a teaspoon of brandy over it. Wrap the cake in waxed paper, but not aluminum foil or plastic wrap, and store in a cool, dry place for at least a week before icing.

| SIZE | QUANTITY* | BAKING TIME |
|---|---|---|
| 6 inch square 7 inch round | half | 1½-2 hours |
| 8 inch square 9 inch round | as given | 3½-4 hours |
| 10 inch square 11 inch round | double | 5½-6 hours |
| 12 inch square 13 inch round | 2½ times | 7½-8 hours |

*refers to the quantity given in the recipe on p. 23.

# WHAT CAN GO WRONG

Knowing how to test a cake correctly is a simple but invaluable skill.

Because a cake bakes from the outside in, it is the center of the cake that you need to test to see if it is done. If you cut a cake and find that the inside is paler, this means that it is not baked properly. You should be able to tell if a cake is baked by gently pressing it with your finger. If the cake springs back, it is done.

A simple, but infallible test for a fruit cake is the skewer test. Insert a skewer in the center of the cake and leave it there for 5 seconds. If it comes out clean, the cake is cooked. If you do not leave the skewer for 5 seconds, it will come out clean whether the cake is cooked or not.

You can also test a sponge cake to see if it is done with a skewer. Stick the skewer into the center of the cake, and if it comes out clean, the cake is done. But take care, because sticking a skewer into a sponge cake or Genoese cake can make it collapse.

### FRUIT CAKE

This fruit cake has not risen properly because it contains too much flour and the ingredients were too cold to start with. The top is scorched for one of three reasons – it was not covered with paper, the oven was too hot or the cake was too near the top of the oven.

### FRUIT CAKE

This cake is a real disaster. It was cooked too quickly at too high a temperature, so that the surface was burned while the inside of the cake remained raw. When it was turned out of the pan it collapsed, because the inside was still soft. This happens when you turn your oven up and forget to lower the temperature when you put the cake in. The top burns, you think the cake is baked, and you take it out too soon.

### SPONGE CAKE

This sponge cake was turned out on to a wire rack. The cake is imprinted with the pattern of the rack, and some of it has stuck and pulled away from the cake.

The cake has not risen because the oven was too hot – the leavening agent was cooked before it could work.

### SPONGE CAKE

This sponge cake has not risen well. There is too much egg in it and the ingredients were too cold to start with.

# COVERING AND FILLING CAKES

There are four basic cake coverings: simple glacé icing, royal icing, fondant icing (also called sugar paste) and buttercream, all of which are included in this section.

Royal icing is the traditional British cake covering. It is a meringue mixture, made with egg white and sugar and beaten until it is aerated. In Australia a new softer icing, sugar paste or cold fondant, is very popular, while Americans have opted for buttercream, which we use both to top our cakes and to sandwich them together. Buttercream is too sweet for some palates, but cake decorators from different countries are now showing a keen interest in each other's cake decorating techniques and ideas are being swapped around the world.

Fondant icing provides a softer, more molded look than the classical style of formal royal icing. It also differs from glacé icing, which is warmed up and poured over a cake and is ideal for the informal decoration of simple sponge cakes. Royal icing has to be applied in several thin coats, and time allowed for drying between coats. If your time is limited, therefore, use fondant icing. A recipe for gelatin icing, which is mainly used for modeling but can be used for covering, is also included in this section.

# MARZIPAN AND ALMOND PASTE

The difference between marzipan and almond paste is in the proportion of almonds used. Marzipan has to have at least 25 per cent almonds – anything less than this and it is called almond paste. Neither uses nuts other than almonds.

Marzipan has been used for centuries by confectioners. Its name means 'the bread of Mars'. It should be smooth and as malleable as potter's clay. It can be used in baking, in macaroons and cookies, for covering and filling cakes, and for making marzipan petits fours and colorful cake decorations.

Marzipan can be nutty white or yellow in color. Traditionally bakers use artificially colored yellow marzipan for wedding cakes, because it looks as good and rich as egg yolk. Today, naturally colored white marzipan is becoming more popular as many cooks prefer not to use artificial coloring. Commercial marzipan is made by blanching and pounding the almonds, and passing them several times through granite rollers. The almonds and sugar are then roasted together.

## UNCOOKED MARZIPAN

This traditional marzipan tends to be oily and crumbly, a little like short pastry, when you roll it out. Because it is uncooked, it is not advisable to store it for more than two or three days before use. If you do have to store it, wrap it in plastic wrap, and put it in a cool part of the refrigerator. You can also freeze it for up to six months. If you are using uncooked marzipan to cover a cake which is to be kept, add a tablespoon of alcohol to act as a preservative.

### INGREDIENTS
2 cups superfine sugar, sifted
3⅓ cups confectioner's sugar, sifted
3½ cups finely ground almonds
1 tbsp rum, brandy or whisky or a few drops of lemon juice or orange flavoured extract
2 large or 3 small eggs (or 4 yolks only)

This quantity makes sufficient for a generous covering on a 9-inch round cake.

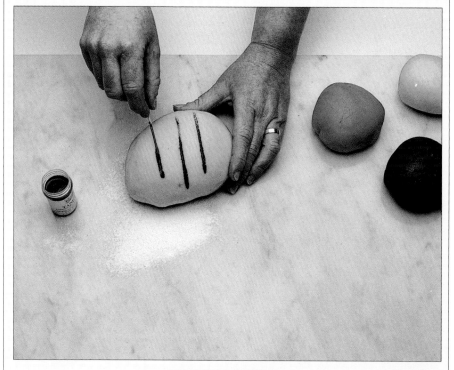

1 Combine the two sugars. Add the ground almonds and mix thoroughly. Make a well in the center and add the rum or other flavoring.

*continued overleaf*

### COLORING MARZIPAN

It is easier to color white marzipan than the commercially produced yellow variety. The artificial yellow coloring distorts some food colors, in particular purple, which tends to become a dull brown color.

Add a very small amount of liquid or paste food color to white marzipan. Dip a wooden pick in the food color and streak the marzipan. Knead the marzipan thoroughly until the color is evenly distributed.

With practice you will soon be able to judge how much color needs to be added to produce a particular shade.

Colored marzipan is used mainly for modeling work (see the sections on marzipan animals, fruit and Christmas decorations on pp. 64-9).

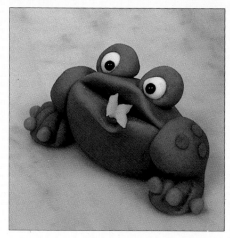

**2** Gradually add the lightly beaten eggs and stir with a wooden spoon or metal spatula to form a stiff paste. You may not need all the egg. If the paste is too soft, it will be difficult to handle.

**3** Gather the mixture together with your hands and knead until it is well combined.

**4** Knead lightly on a sugared counter until smooth. Avoid over-kneading, or it may become greasy.

**5** The finished result – an evenly textured and malleable paste. Store it in an airtight container or a double wrapping of plastic wrap.

## COOKED ALMOND PASTE

This is a quick-drying paste that is not oily. It keeps well for several weeks in the refrigerator but, if possible, make it about 24 hours before it is required. Store it in an airtight container or a double wrapping of plastic wrap. If it dries, moisten it with a little egg white.

### INGREDIENTS

2 cups sugar
⅔ cup plus 4 tbsp water
large pinch of cream of tartar
2½ cups finely ground almonds
2 egg whites

**1** Combine the sugar and milk in a saucepan and bring it to the boil over medium heat, stirring. Beating constantly, slowly pour syrup in thin steady stream over yolks and blend thoroughly. Pour back into saucepan and cook over low heat until thickened – do not allow to boil.

**2** When the sugar has completely dissolved, add the cream of tartar and bring the syrup to the boil. Boil rapidly without stirring until it reaches soft ball (240°F on a candy thermometer).

**3** Stop the boiling process quickly by plunging the base of the saucepan into a bowl of cold water. Stir in the ground almonds.

**4** Stir in the egg whites. Return the pan to a low heat and stir until the paste thickens slightly.

**5** Turn the paste out onto a marble slab, counter or wooden board sprinkled with confectioner's sugar and work it with a metal spatula until it begins to cool and thicken.

**6** As you work the paste, sprinkle over a dusting of sifted confectioner's sugar, to prevent it sticking to the counter.

**7** When it gets cool enough, knead it with your hands. It will take up to half its weight in confectioner's sugar. The finished paste should feel dry to the touch. Do not add too much sugar at a time or the mixture will become too dry and will crumble when rolled out or worked. The more sugar you add, the harder you will have to work to disperse the oils produced by the almonds.

**8** Store the cooked almond paste in an airtight jar or thick plastic bag.

# FILLINGS AND TOPPINGS

The recipes in this section are easy to make and are ideal for filling and decorating cakes for a simple occasion or if time is short. They include several variations on buttercream, frostings, crème pâtissière and pralines.

## BUTTERCREAM

Buttercream is a simple combination of butter and sugar, beaten together to lighten it and eliminate any greasiness. It can be used for both filling and topping cakes. The butter should be pale colored and unsalted.

### INGREDIENTS
½ cup unsalted butter
1⅓ cups confectioner's sugar, sifted
flavoring (see below)

**1** Warm the butter in a bowl. Beat it with a whisk until it is light and fluffy and then gradually add the confectioner's sugar, until it is all incorporated. An electric mixer will save you a lot of hard work here. Alternatively use a balloon whisk to begin with to get the butter fluffy and then a rotary whisk for incorporating the sugar.

**2** The finished buttercream is thicker and stiffer than whipped cream, but light and very pale.

**3** Buttercream can be left plain or flavored with vanilla, lemon, orange, chocolate, coffee, mocha or mint. To flavor it with chocolate, as here, mix in cooled melted chocolate, which gives a smoother taste and finish than adding unsweetened cocoa powder.

### FLAVORINGS

These should be beaten into the finished buttercream until well blended.
*Vanilla* ½ teaspoon vanilla extract.
*Lemon* 1 teaspoon lemon juice with a little finely grated zest. Do not use the zest if the buttercream is to be piped.
*Orange* ½ tablespoon orange juice with a little finely grated zest.
*Chocolate* 1 tablespoon unsweetened cocoa powder or 2 ounces cooled melted chocolate.
*Coffee* 1 heaped teaspoon instant coffee dissolved in ½ teaspoon hot water.
*Mocha* 1 teaspoon unsweetened cocoa powder and 1 teaspoon instant coffee.
*Mint* 2 drops peppermint oil with a little green food coloring.

## CREME AU BEURRE

Crème au beurre will keep in the refrigerator for a week or two, but must be brought to room temperature and re-beaten before being used.

### INGREDIENTS
8 oz sugar lumps
⅓ cup water
pinch of cream of tartar
6 egg yolks
1½ cups unsalted butter

**1** Put the sugar, water and cream of tartar in a saucepan and stir over a low heat until the sugar has completely dissolved. Wash the sides of the pan with a pastry brush dipped in cold water, to make sure no crystals are left sticking to it. Raise the heat and boil rapidly without stirring until the syrup reaches 240°F on a candy thermometer.

**2** While the syrup is cooking, beat the egg yolks until they are fluffy. Then, beating constantly, pour the boiled syrup in a thin stream on to the yolks. The mixture will become thick and light as it cools. Leave to cool completely.

**3** Beat the butter to a light creamy consistency, then beat in the sugar and yolk mixture.

## CUSTARD BUTTERCREAM

### INGREDIENTS
¼ cup sugar
⅔ cup milk
2 egg yolks, well beaten
¾-1 cup unsalted butter
flavoring

**1** Put the sugar with the milk in a pan and bring it to the boil, stirring. Pour it on to the yolks, blend and return to the pan. Thicken over a gentle heat, but do not boil.

**2** Warm the butter to room temperature and cream well, then whip in the custard a little at a time.

**3** Flavor the cream to taste with coffee flavoring, lemon or orange zest, or chocolate. For chocolate crème au beurre, beat ½ cup melted and cooled semi-sweet chocolate and 3-4 tablespoons cognac into the finished cream.

## EUROPEAN BUTTERCREAM

This is cold boiled custard mixed with creamed butter. Either use packaged custard (Bird's English dessert mix) or follow the recipe below, which is light but rich in flavor.

### INGREDIENTS
1¼ cups milk
¾ cup superfine sugar
6 egg yolks
1 egg
1½ cups unsalted butter

**1** Put all the ingredients except the butter in a double boiler and whip over a low heat until the custard coats the back of a wooden spoon. Pour the custard into a cold bowl and leave to cool.

*continued overleaf*

**2** Beat the butter until it is pale and fluffy, then beat in the cold custard.

## AMERICAN BUTTERCREAM

### INGREDIENTS
1 cup butter (or half butter, half margarine), room temperature
⅔ cup milk
½ tsp salt
2 tsp vanilla extract (or rose water or orange flavoured extract)
6⅔ cups confectioner's sugar, sifted

**1** Combine the butter, milk, salt, vanilla and half the sugar in a mixing bowl and blend gently. Gradually add the remaining sugar and continue beating until light and fluffy.

**2** Add flavorings, extracts, colorings or liqueurs as desired. Cover with a damp cloth and keep in a cool place until ready to use.

## BAVARIAN CHOCOLATE CREAM

### INGREDIENTS
1¼ cups milk
3 tbsp superfine sugar
1 ounce semisweet chocolate
1 egg
2 egg yolks
2 tsp cornstarch
a few drops of vanilla extract
2 tbsp milk
1 envelope gelatin
⅔ cup whipping cream (optional)
1 tbsp superfine sugar (optional)

**1** Combine the milk, sugar and chocolate in a saucepan and bring it to boil stirring over a medium heat.

**2** In another saucepan mix the egg, yolks, cornstarch and vanilla. Remove from heat. Add the milk mixture and stir over a gentle heat until thickened.

**3** Warm the remaining milk and dissolve the gelatin in it, then stir this into the custard and allow to cool.

**4** For a richer cream, beat ⅔ cup whipping cream with 1 tbsp superfine sugar until fairly stiff, then fold it gently into the cooled custard.

*The buttercreams illustrated here are (counterclockwise from top): Chocolate crème au beurre (p. 29), European buttercream (p. 29) and American buttercream (p. 30). The cake is decorated with the Chocolate crème au beurre, toasted walnuts and chocolate shavings.*

## AMERICAN FROSTING

American frosting is very white because it is made with vegetable shortening. You can disguise the taste of the shortening with a little orange flavored extract. Do not add a colored flavoring, such as vanilla, or the icing will go brown.

### INGREDIENTS
3⅓ cups powdered sugar sifted
¾ cup vegetable shortening
⅓ cup milk
½ tsp salt
½ tsp orange flavored extract

**1** Combine half the sugar in a medium bowl with the remaining ingredients. Begin mixing at a low speed to avoid having the sugar sprayed all over the kitchen. Scrape the bowl down frequently to get all the sugar off the sides.

**2** As the frosting becomes thick and creamy slowly add the rest of the sugar and continue beating until the frosting is light and fluffy.

## SEVEN-MINUTE FROSTING

### INGREDIENTS
¾ cup superfine sugar
2 tbsp water
1 tsp light corn syrup
pinch of salt
1 egg white
flavoring

**1** Combine the sugar, water, corn syrup, salt and egg white in the top of a double boiler and heat gently over direct heat until the sugar has dissolved.

**2** Set over boiling water and beat the mixture for 7 minutes with a rotary beater until it stands in soft peaks.

**3** Remove from the heat and continue beating until the frosting is thick enough to spread.

## GINGER CREAM FILLING

### INGREDIENTS
1¼ cups confectioner's custard (see p. 34)
⅓ cup preserved ginger
grated lemon zest, finely sliced
2-3 tsp ginger syrup
2 tbsp whipped cream

**1** Combine the custard, ginger and lemon zest in a bowl. Stir in the ginger syrup and fold in the cream.

**2** If the filling is too thin, add some cake crumbs. Pineapple may be substituted for ginger.

## CREME PATISSIERE

### INGREDIENTS
2 egg yolks
3 tbsp all-purpose flour
1 ½ tbsp cornstarch
¼ cup superfine sugar
1 ¼ cups milk
1 egg white
3 or 4 drops vanilla extract

This quantity is sufficient for filling and topping an 8-inch sponge cake.

**1** Lightly beat yolks in a small bowl. Add the sugar gradually and cream well. Sift flour and cornstarch together. Beat into mixture along with half of the milk.

**2** Bring the remaining milk to the boil. Slowly stir it into the egg mixture and blend well. Return mixture to the milk pan and stir over medium heat until the mixture reaches boiling point. Set aside.

**3** Beat the egg white until stiff. Take about a quarter of the blended cream from the pan and fold the beaten egg white gently into it. Then return the mixture to the pan and cook over a gentle heat for 3 to 4 minutes, folding the mixture occasionally and adding the vanilla. Turn it into a bowl to cool.

## GOLDEN PRALINE

Golden praline is coarser textured and more crunchy than white praline. Praline can be used on the sides and tops of cakes or for a filling.

### INGREDIENTS
½ cup superfine sugar
⅔ cup blanched whole almonds

**1** Put the sugar and almonds into a pan and stir over a very low heat until the sugar melts. Allow the mixture to cook, stirring occasionally to prevent sticking, until it is a rich golden brown.

**2** Pour it on to an oiled marble slab and let it cool. When it is cold, crush the nuts with a rolling pin.

## WHITE PRALINE

### INGREDIENTS
6 oz sugar cubes
¼ cup water
½ cup finely ground almonds

**1** In a heavy, small saucepan dissolve the sugar lumps in the water stirring frequently until the syrup boils. Boil without stirring until 248°-258°F on a candy thermometer. Turn off the heat.

*continued on p. 34*

**2** Stir in the ground almonds until you have a crumbly consistency. Rub the nuts through a sieve and store in an airtight container until needed.

**2** Stir in the egg yolks and flavoring. Do not be tempted to add the yolks before the custard has cooled, as they will curdle and start to cook.

## CONFECTIONER'S CUSTARD

### INGREDIENTS

1 ¼ cups milk
2 tbsp cornstarch
2 egg yolks
2 tbsp superfine sugar
½ tsp vanilla extract

**1** In a small saucepan warm the milk gently. Blend in the cornstarch. Bring to the boil, stirring, and simmer for 5 minutes. Remove from the heat and let cool.

**3** Stir in the sugar, return to the heat and cook gently for a few minutes, without allowing it to boil. Once the sugar has dissolved, cover the pan and let cool.

*Confectioner's custard and whipped cream* BELOW *make lavish fillings and toppings. The cake is filled and decorated with piped whipped cream, candied fruit, almonds and chocolate sprinkles.*

# GELATIN ICING

Gelatin icing is mainly used for modeling work, as an alternative to modeling paste or petal paste (see p. 72). It is used in several of the fantasy cakes in Section 2.

When you are ready to start using the icing, work with it quickly, as it sets rapidly and shaping can become difficult even after a minute. Always keep the icing you are not using tightly wrapped in plastic wrap.

### INGREDIENTS
¼ cup water
2 envelopes unflavored gelatin powder
2 tsp light corn syrup
3⅓ cups powdered sugar sifted
cornstarch

**1** Put the water in a small bowl and add the gelatin. Let soak for 2 minutes.

**2** Place the bowl in an ovenproof pan containing ½ inch of water, and put the pan over direct heat.

**3** Heat the water to simmering, stirring constantly until all the lumps have dissolved and the liquid is clear. Remove the bowl from the pan and let cool for 1 minute.

**4** Add the corn syrup to the gelatin mixture and stir until dissolved. Let cool for 2 minutes.

**5** Place the sugar in a mixing bowl, then add the gelatin mixture and stir with a wooden spoon. If the mixture is a little wet, add more powdered sugar.

**6** Stir sufficient cornstarch in to the mixture in order to allow the icing to be worked like bread dough.

**7** To store the icing wrap it tightly in a plastic bag. Any air coming into contact with the surface of the icing will cause it to get dry and hard, making it impossible to use.

### COLORING GELATIN ICING

If the icing is to be colored, the color can be added to the warm gelatin mixture making it easier to incorporate into the icing. However, adding the color in advance does mean that the color may be darker than you had expected.

# GLACE ICING

Glacé icing is simply and quickly made from powdered sugar and warm water. No cooking is involved. It is most suitable for sponge cakes, small cakes and iced petits fours. It sets very quickly and must be used while still warm.

## GLACE ICING

### INGREDIENTS

1 scant cup powdered sugar
1¼ tbsp warm water
flavoring and coloring as required

This quantity will cover a 7-inch cake or about 18 small cup cakes.

**1** Sift the confectioner's sugar into a bowl and beat in the warm water a little at a time until the desired consistency is reached.

**2** The consistency of glacé icing is important. It should be just thick enough to coat the back of a spoon so that it pours evenly on to the cake.

**3** Add your chosen coloring and flavoring. Coloring paste is better than liquid color because it does not affect the consistency of the icing. Paste colors are much stronger and more vibrant than the liquid varieties. They should be added sparingly with a wooden pick.

## RICH ORANGE ICING

### INGREDIENTS

¾ cup powdered sugar, sifted
juice of 1 orange
1 tbsp simple syrup (see below) or water

**1** Combine the powdered sugar and orange juice in a small pan over low heat and mix in the syrup or water to a creamy consistency. (Use syrup if possible because it gives a richer gloss to the finished icing than water.)

**2** Pour over the cake. Candied orange peel softened in hot water makes an attractive decoration.

## REAL CHOCOLATE ICING

Real chocolate icing is luxuriously rich. If it gets too stiff, you can either beat it over a pan of warm, but not hot, water or add simple syrup (see below).

### INGREDIENTS

1 cup semi-sweet chocolate chips or
   3 oz semisweet chocolate squares
½ cup unsalted butter, cut into pieces
1 tbsp light corn syrup
2-3 tsp brandy or water

**1** Combine the chocolate, butter and corn syrup in a double boiler or a bowl over hot water and stir until smooth and completely melted.

**2** Add the brandy or water and stir. Remove from the heat and allow to cool until almost set but still spreadable.

## FUDGE ICING

This is a soft textured icing that can be used unthickened to pour over the cakes or thickened and shaped into informal patterns with a knife or serrated spatula.

### INGREDIENTS

1⅔ cups powdered sugar
3 tbsp butter or margarine
2 tbsp milk or cream
pinch of salt
3 drops vanilla extract

This amount will cover the top and sides of a 7-inch cake. If a filling is required as well, double the quantity.

**1** Sift the powdered sugar into a bowl. Melt the butter or margarine in a small saucepan. Do not allow it to boil or it will separate. Add the milk or cream and salt and heat gently to just below simmering point. Keep it at this temperature for 2 minutes, then add the vanilla. Pour the mixture over the sugar and beat until stiff.

**2** To coat the top and sides of the cake, pour the icing over quickly just as it is beginning to stiffen. If you want to make a pattern in the icing, beat it for a little longer before coating the cake.

### SIMPLE SYRUP

This syrup can be used to thin down any icing or fondant that has become too stiff to work with easily.

### INGREDIENTS

4 cups sugar
2½ cups water

In a heavy saucepan boil the sugar and water to the thread (215°-200°F on a candy thermometer), stirring until there are no crystals left. Skim while boiling.

*A filling of Crème pâtissière provides a sweet contrast to the tang of Rich Orange icing ABOVE OPPOSITE. Real chocolate icing BELOW OPPOSITE can be made from chocolate squares or chocolate chips.*

# ROYAL ICING

Working with royal icing is the single most important aspect of cake decorating. It is used both for piping and for covering the cake.

Royal icing, or glacé royale, as it is also known, is made by beating together sugar and egg whites. The action of beating incorporates millions of minute air bubbles into the mixture, and it is this that gives it its texture. Well made royal icing can be easily cut with a sharp knife.

The slightest trace of egg yolk or grease, however, will break down the egg white and prevent it from becoming properly aerated, no matter how much you beat it. One solution is to keep the bowl and other equipment you use for making royal icing for that purpose alone. Alternatively, you can make sure your bowl is grease-free by washing it out with hot, soapy water, rinsing it under hot water and then standing it upside down to drain. Let it dry off by itself. If you need to dry it quickly, use a freshly laundered tea towel.

Never beat royal icing in a plastic bowl, because you may scrape tiny slivers of plastic off it as you beat. If you transfer the icing to a plastic bowl in order to store it, again make sure the bowl is completely grease-free.

## MAKING ROYAL ICING BY HAND

Royal icing made by hand often has a better consistency than that made in a mixer, because you can judge by the feel of it when to add more sugar and when the icing is ready.

### INGREDIENTS
1 egg white, room temperature
about 2½ cups powdered sugar, sifted
   twice just before using
strained juice of half a lemon

If the icing is to be used for coating the cake only, weigh out the correct amount and put it in a clean bowl, then add 1 teaspoon glycerine per 1½ cups. This will help to give an icing that will cut without splintering.

**1** Break up the egg white with a metal spatula making sure that both the spatula and the bowl are free from grease. A metal spatula cuts and aerates the white more effectively than a metal spoon.

**2** Very gradually add the finely sifted sugar, working each addition in well with the metal spatula before adding the next. Only add half a tablespoon at a time. If you add it too quickly and do not beat it enough in between additions, the result will be too much sugar in the icing, and this will give it a

---

### ROYAL ICING INGREDIENTS

**Egg white**
It is a good idea to break and separate the eggs you are going to use for royal icing two or three hours before making it, or even the night before. This will allow some of the water to evaporate from the white, which increases its viscosity and makes a stronger icing.

Reconstituted albumen powder can be substituted for fresh egg white in royal icing. Use it according to the manufacturer's instructions, but the ratio is generally 1½ tbsp albumen powder to ⅓ cup water to 3⅓ cups sugar.

Separate the egg white or albumen mixture into a grease-free bowl and cover it with a dampened cloth to prevent it completely drying out.

**Sugar**
The amount of powdered sugar you need is impossible to specify exactly, because it depends on the quantity of egg white. Sift the sugar twice through a fine sieve, or it may block decorating tips and cause you a great deal of frustration.

**Additives**
Some people add a little acetic acid or cream of tartar to royal icing to increase its frothing power and to strengthen it. Be careful not to add too much, or it will give the sugar a strong pungent odor, spoil the color and harden the icing. Adding a squeeze of lemon juice both whitens the icing and gives it more elasticity. This is useful while you are working with the icing, but once it has set the lemon juice tends to make it more brittle and liable to crack when you cut the cake. Therefore, only add lemon juice to icing which is to be used for piping, but not for covering the cake.

If you use an additive in the covering icing, be sure to use exactly the same amount if you make a second batch of icing, otherwise the result will be patchy.

If you find the icing very hard and splintery when you cut the cake, it is because not enough air has been incorporated into it by beating. Some cake decorators add 1 teaspoon glycerine per 3⅓ cups powdered sugar. This will make the icing a little softer. Only add glycerine to icing for covering the cake, not for piping.

Never add more than the proportion of glycerine given above, or you will prevent proper drying of the icing coatings. This can have disastrous results if, for example, the weight of an upper tier of a cake concentrated on the pillars slips to overly-moist icing.

dull yellowish color. Stir frequently round the sides of the bowl to incorporate the sugar sticking to it, and every time you do so, scrape off the knife on the edge of the bowl to stop sugar building up on the blade. If you do not do this, the unincorporated crystals will harden in the air and cause blockages in the decorating tips.

3 As you add more sugar the syrup thickens until you can pull it into a peak when you lift the knife out of it. Once the icing is stiff enough to hold a peak, add a squeeze of lemon juice. If this wets the icing too much, incorporate a little more sugar. The lemon juice will give the icing a smoother, creamier feel. Remember that a firmer consistency·is needed for piping borders and a softer consistency for line work.

4 To store the icing, you must protect it from moisture. Carefully wipe off the sides of the bowl with a clean cloth to remove every particle of sugar.

5 Take a piece of plastic wrap and press it right down on to the icing, smoothing it to eliminate any air bubbles. Put another layer of plastic wrap across the top of the bowl and seal the bowl in an airtight container. You can store it in this way for up to two weeks. Do not put the icing in the refrigerator because it will absorb moisture, and this spoils its consistency.

## MAKING ROYAL ICING IN A MIXER

You can also make royal icing in a mixer. It will save you a lot of hard work, but you will not be able to judge the consistency with the same accuracy. Always keep the beater on the lowest speed – if you beat it fast you will incorporate too much air into it and large bubbles may appear as you ice the cake.

The basic principle is the same as for making the icing by hand. The following photographs show the technique using dried egg powder – pure albumen – egg substitute, or a boosted albumen.

### INGREDIENTS
3⅓ cups sugar, sifted twice
⅓ cup water
1½ tbsp or 7 tsp albumen powder

1 First mix the water and albumen into a small bowl. The resulting liquid will be sloppy and lumpy and give off a strong smell. Do not give up and throw it away! Albumen does have a strong smell. It has a very long shelf life and the smell does not mean it has gone bad. Do not try to whip out the lumps of coagulated albumen. Let it stand for at least 15 minutes, or a couple of hours, or overnight if possible, to dissolve.

2 Sieve the albumen and water mixture into the mixing bowl. Add half the sugar and beat it until you have a smooth consistency, remembering to wipe down the sides of the bowl frequently to incorporate any sugar that may be sticking to it. Then add the rest of the sugar and, if you are using pure albumen, beat it for 12-14 minutes. If you are using boosted albumen, you should reach the right consistency after beating for only about 4 minutes. Boosted albumen contains a foaming agent that helps it reach the right consistency much quicker than normal egg white, and therefore it needs less beating. If you overbeat it, your icing will be very hard and splintery.

3 When the right consistency is reached, when it can stand up in soft peaks, seal and store the icing as for handmade icing.

### COLORING ROYAL ICING

It is difficult to achieve strong royal icing colors, such as Christmas red, royal blue, moss green or black, with the standard food colors widely available in general stores. Better colors are achieved with food colors designed for the purpose available from specialist cake decorating sources.

Food colors come in several forms – as liquid, powder, syrup or paste. Powder is not recommended as it is extremely messy to use. Both paste and liquid colors maintain the consistency of the royal icing, and are the most suitable.

In order to achieve a bright red or true black, it is important to allow the color to 'wet out' in the icing – that is, to let the icing stand for 20-30 minutes while the color strength develops.

# FONDANT ICING

Fondant is used for both icing cakes and making cake decorations. It has a softer, more molded look than the more stiffly formal royal icing, and is becoming increasingly popular among cake decorators.

## UNCOOKED FONDANT

Uncooked fondant is the easiest fondant to make. It works reasonably well, though it does not have the elasticity or fine texture of cooked fondant. It rolls out rather like short pastry. It can be made by hand or in a mixer. Do not use a hand-held mixer as it may not be strong enough.

### INGREDIENTS
2 tbsp light corn syrup
1 egg white
5-6½ cups powdered sugar, sifted
juice of half a lemon
1½ tsp glycerine
flavoring and coloring as required

**1** Soften the corn syrup over hot water. Put the egg white into a mixing bowl, add about half the confectioner's sugar and beat well until the mixture begins to stiffen. Add the lemon juice and beat again.

**2** Add about 1⅔ cups powdered sugar to the mixture. Beat thoroughly until all the sugar is well incorporated.

**3** Add the glycerine and corn syrup and continue beating in more sugar until the mixture has thickened. Incorporate the flavoring.

**4** Once the paste is stiff, sift some powdered sugar on to a counter. Tip out the mixture onto it and knead it, adding more sugar, until it loses all signs of stickiness.

**5** Test to see if the paste is ready by pressing it firmly with your fingers. If your fingers are sticky, you need to add more sugar.

**6** This fondant can be used straight away, but it is better to leave it overnight before coating the cake. Wrap it tightly in a double layer of plastic wrap and seal it in an airtight container.

## EUROPEAN FONDANT ICING

This is a superb fondant, but quite difficult to make. You will need a marble slab and plenty of muscle power – a good half hour's work is involved. If you do not feel quite strong enough for European fondant, try the less strenuous Australian fondant which follows.

### INGREDIENTS
2 cups sugar
1 tbsp light corn syrup
⅔ cup water

**1** Wet the marble slab. Combine the sugar and corn syrup in a saucepan. To measure out corn syrup by the tablespoon, either put the jar into a bowl of hot water until it becomes thin and runny or use a very hot spoon to take it from the jar.

**2** Stir in the water over a gentle heat. As you bring the sugar to boiling point, stir continuously with a wooden spoon and wash down the sides of the pan with a dampened pastry brush to stop the sugar reverting to crystals.

**3** When the syrup has reached a temperature of 240°C (called the 'soft ball' stage), plunge the bottom of the saucepan into cold water to stop it cooking further.

### SOFT BALL TEMPERATURE

The best way of testing the temperature is using a special candy thermometer, which is calibrated to about 280°F. Alternatively, use the 'soft ball' test, which involves dropping a teaspoon of the liquid into a cup of water – if the liquid forms a ball, it has reached the right temperature. The disadvantage with this method is that while you are carrying out the test the liquid continues to boil. By the time the test is completed, the syrup may have boiled too much, reducing its water content and making it unusable because it will have started to discolor.

**4** Pour the syrup in a spiral motion from the pan on to the marble slab. Marble is the best surface for the speedy cooling of the syrup. You can use an ordinary counter, but the syrup will take longer to cool.

**5** To aid cooling, sprinkle the syrup with cold water from a pastry brush. As it cools, the syrup turns whitish in color. Do not be tempted to work it before it has cooled or it will become tough and sugary.

**6** When the syrup has completely cooled, take a damp metal scraper and begin lifting the edges of the syrup and folding them in towards the center.

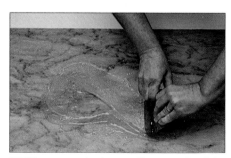

**7** Then work in a figure of eight motion, turning the outside edges of the syrup into the center all the time. Carry on working for about five minutes until it is glossy and viscous and has a creamy-colored tinge.

**8** After a while you will probably find the syrup is easier to stir with a long-handled spatula, so that you can put more pressure on it as you mix.

**9** The mixture will gradually become thick and opaque and you will need to use both hands to continue mixing. At this stage it is often easier to go back to the metal scraper to lift it and turn it.

**10** The mixture will eventually become white and crumbly and too thick to work at all. It will take up to 20 minutes of hard work to get to this point.

**11** Moisten your hands and work the crumbled fondant into a ball. Knead it for five to ten minutes until it is completely smooth and free from lumps. You can complete this process using a food mixer with a dough hook.

**12** Wrap the fondant tightly in plastic wrap and store it in a sealed container in the refrigerator. It will keep for up to four weeks.

This fondant can be used in two ways – either as a cold fondant or a cooked fondant. To make a cold rolled fondant, or sugar paste, add a little powdered sugar to the fondant and simply roll it out to cover a cake.

To make a cooked fondant, which is used for fondant petits fours or fondant centers for chocolates, put the fondant in a double boiler over a low heat to break it down. Add simple syrup (see p. 36) until the consistency has thinned enough to coat the back of a wooden spoon. Now it is ready to use. Pour it over your cake, as you would glacé icing.

## AUSTRALIAN FONDANT ICING

This is a much easier method than the European fondant icing. It makes a good fondant without using a marble slab. Make the fondant at least 24 hours before use.

### INGREDIENTS
¼ cup gelatin
1¼ cups water
2 cups sugar
½ cup (4 oz) light corn syrup
2 tbsp (1 oz) glycerine
1 tsp cream of tartar
½ cup white vegetable shortening
3 lb powdered sugar, sifted

**1** Put the gelatin with half the water in a small bowl and set it in a saucepan of hot water. Stir until it has thoroughly dissolved.

**2** Put the sugar, corn syrup, glycerine, cream of tartar and the remaining ⅔ cup water in a wide heavy saucepan and stir over a medium heat until the sugar has completely dissolved. Brush the sides of the pan down with a dampened pastry brush to stop crystals forming. Without stirring, bring the sugar to the boil and boil over high heat to soft ball – 240°F.

**3** Remove the pan from the heat and put it in a bowl of cold water to cool for three to four minutes. Stir in the white vegetable shortening and add the dissolved gelatin.

**4** Add the powdered sugar a spoonful at a time. Stir after each addition to make sure the sugar has completely dissolved before you add the next quantity.

**5** When you have added all the sugar, the fondant will be a thick paste. Spoon it on to the counter and knead it until it is very smooth and free from lumps.

The fondant should be wrapped tightly in a double layer of plastic wrap and sealed in an airtight container. Store it in the refrigerator for at least 24 hours before you use it. Never let air get to a fondant. It will tend to dry out and it may crack as you put it on the cake. Before you use the fondant, allow it to reach room temperature again. Knead in up to a tablespoon of powdered sugar if necessary to get rid of any stickiness.

# SIMPLE DECORATING
# TECHNIQUES

This section demonstrates the classic decoration of sponge cakes with soft fillings and coatings, including very easy designs with a dusting of confectioner's sugar and more elaborate piped buttercream coverings. If you are a beginner, you will find here an introduction to some of the basic techniques and tools of cake decoration.

The techniques are simple but create attractive effects, and include diamond marking, cobweb icing and feather icing, grooving, swirling and peaking, two ways to decorate a jelly roll and coating sponge cake with soft fondant icing. All the cakes are ideal for everyday or even to celebrate an informal festive occasion. Following these demonstrations will give you practice in using some of the basic tools of the trade – the turntable, metal spatulas, cake combs, pastry bags and food color – and at the same time help you develop your skills.

## EQUIPMENT AND DECORATIONS

The techniques covered in this section require only fairly basic cake decorating equipment. The turntable is the most expensive item illustrated here, but if you are planning to take up cake decorating, it is worth having from the very beginning.

1 *A heavy-duty metal turntable. Cheaper models are available in plastic.*
2 *Food paste colors*
3 *Crystallized violets*
4 *Crystallized rose petals*
5 *Angelica*
6 *Candied cherries*
7 *Piped sugar flowers*
8 *Real chocolate sprinkles*
9 *Silver and colored balls or dragees*
10 *Pastry bag stand, with two filled pastry bags and tips*
11 *Thick paintbrushes, for cleaning up around a partially finished cake*
12 *12-inch spatula*
13 *4-inch metal spatula*
14 *Stainless steel rolling pin*
15 *Stainless steel profiled-edge scraper, for special effects on the side of a cake*
16 *Plastic scraper, for 'combing' the side of a cake*
17 *Parchment pastry bag triangles*

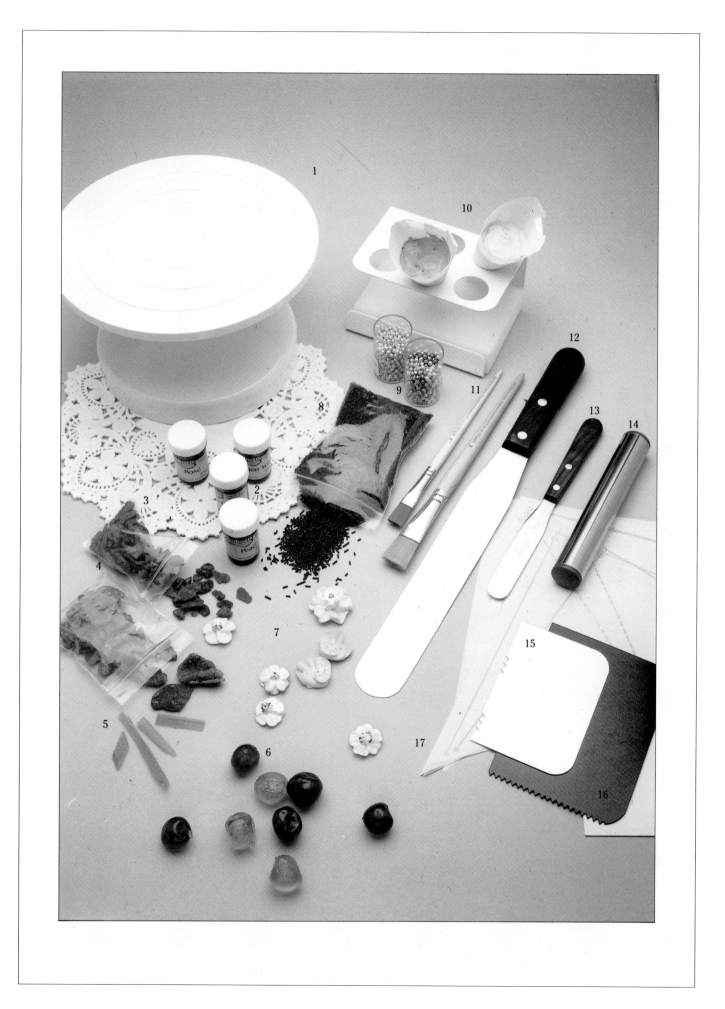

# NUT AND COCONUT DECORATION

Nuts and coconut are widely used in simple cake decoration, particularly in combination with buttercream, whipped cream and glacé icing. Their flavor and texture contrast well with sweet, soft toppings and fillings. They also make very attractive decorations. Illustrated here are a variety of ground and whole nuts, blanched and unblanched almonds, and plain and colored coconut.

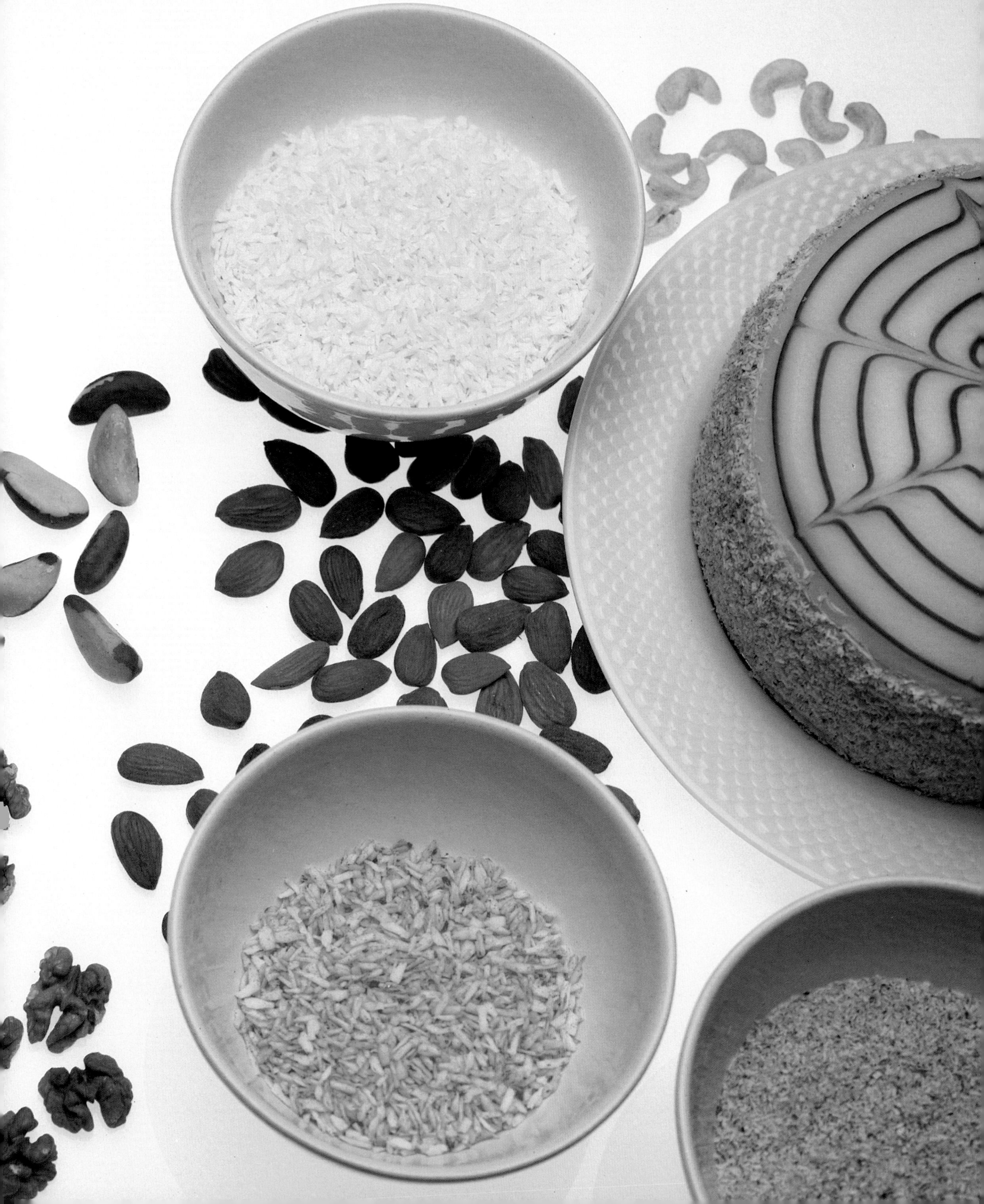

# DECORATING SPONGE CAKES

## FILLING

A Victoria sponge cake is traditionally filled with whipped cream and jam, either strawberry or raspberry, for a good contrast.

Spread one half of the cake with cream, and the other with jam, using a metal spatula. Do not try to spread them one on top of the other. Sandwich the two halves together.

## DUSTING

**1** For a very pretty dusting on top of the cake, cover it with a paper doily and gently tap confectioner's sugar from a sieve on to the cake.

**2** Remove the doily very carefully or you will spoil the pattern beneath. Use this technique, too, with home-made stencils. If you are giving the cake as a present for example, you can stencil the person's name over the top.

## COATING THE SIDES OF THE CAKE

Buttercream makes a very good coating for the sides of a sponge cake. It is particularly useful for a layer cake because it covers the joint and gives a smooth finish. The cake can then be rolled in silver balls, chocolate sprinkles, chopped nuts, granola or finely chopped candied fruit.

**1** Smooth the buttercream round the sides of the cake with a metal spatula.

**2** Fill your palm with chopped nuts or golden praline and brush the nuts against the buttercream all round the base of the cake.

**3** If you want to coat the sides of the cake completely, spread a layer of the decoration (here, chocolate sprinkles) on a sheet of wax paper and roll the cake in it, holding it flat between your palms.

## GLACE ICING

Glacé icing can be colored and flavored. If you use a flavoring that is slightly colored, use a coloring as well, or the result may be an unattractive off-white. Lemon juice heightens the whiteness of glacé icing. Orange flavored extract, peppermint oil and rose water are flavorings which will not discolor glacé icing.

**1** To coat the top of the cake with glacé icing, carefully pour the icing out of the bowl, keeping up a steady stream. Stop as it ripples out to the edge, and smooth it if necessary with a dry metal spatula. Tap the cake on the counter to flatten and settle the icing.

**2** If you want to decorate glacé icing, have your decoration at hand, because it sets quickly. Put the cake on its display plate straight away – the icing may craze if the cake is moved after it has dried.

---

### HANDY HINT

Remember if the top of the cake is not perfect, you can turn it upside down and use the flat base for the top.

---

*The cake OPPOSITE features chocolate sprinkles around the base, a piped rope of Bavarian buttercream around the edge, and segments of crystallized orange on the top. Simple decorations such as these can make something special out of the plainest cake.*

## ROSETTES

The sides and top of this cake have been decorated with buttercream, combed with a serrated comb and a strip of golden praline laid around the base. The spiral effect on the top has been made by putting the cake on a turntable and holding a metal spatula over it like the arm of a record player while the cake is rotated.

1 To make rosettes, fill a large pastry bag with buttercream and use star tip No. 15. Pipe the rosettes in a circular motion, one at a time – if you try to pipe them continuously, they will turn into scrolls.

2 Finish decorating the cake with green candied cherries, cut into segments and positioned on the sides between the rosettes. Make a flower shape of candied pineapple with a yellow candied cherry for its center on the top.

## PEAKING

1 Cover the top of the cake with butter-icing and use a metal spatula to pull it up into peaks.

2 Sprinkle the top with colored sprinkles and add a gold ribbon for a festive effect.

## DIAMOND MARKING

1 Cover the sides of the cake with chocolate sprinkles and spread the top with chocolate buttercream. Make a diamond pattern by pulling a skewer through the buttercream as shown.

2 Pipe simple shells round the edge of the top of the cake using star tip No. 11 or 12 and chocolate buttercream.

*Simple decorating techniques can produce attractive results – the cake RIGHT is decorated with a serrated comb and piped rosettes; the chocolate cake BELOW is diamond marked with a border of piped shells.*

## SWIRLING

**1** You can use a cake comb to create all sorts of patterns in butter icing. Hold the comb against the side of the cake as you rotate it on a turntable, or move it from left to right across the top to make waves, as here.

**2** Pipe stars round the edge of the cake and finish if off with a white satin ribbon.

## GROOVING

**1** Use a cake comb with chocolate buttercream to create this complicated looking effect very simply. Rotate the cake on a turntable and move the comb sideways to make undulations. Be careful when you get back to the beginning of your pattern not to make a ridge. Use a deeply grooved comb on the sides of the cake.

**2** Pipe a rosette in the center, and beading around the top and bottom edges of the cake.

*Always make a generous quantity of buttercream when decorating cakes like this one BELOW. A lot of buttercream is scraped off as the pattern is made.*

## COBWEB ICING

**1** Pour the fondant over the top of the cake. Pipe concentric circles of chocolate icing, fondant or melted chocolate on the fondant. Start from the center and work outwards. When the circles are completed, draw a skewer across the cake from the center outwards, dividing it into quarters. Draw the skewer from the edge of the cake inwards, dividing it into eighths.

**2** Hold the cake in the palms of your hands and roll the sides in green colored coconut.

## FEATHER ICING

Feathering is an attractive way of finishing off glacé icing or fondant. Fondant is used here. It takes slightly longer to set and gives you more time to work.

**1** Pour the fondant over the top of the cake. The cake can have a marzipan base. Pipe straight lines of chocolate icing, fondant or melted chocolate across the cake. The best way of keeping the lines parallel is by working form the center outwards. Starting at the center of the cake, draw a skewer through the lines in the opposite direction, leaving a double space

*To color coconut as for the cobweb-iced cake ABOVE, rub a little food color on to your fingers and work them through the coconut. This method gives a good even color.*

between the lines. Turn the cake round and repeat the process in the other direction creating a feather pattern.

**2** Roll the sides of the cake in green colored coconut and pipe a line of chocolate shells round the edge of the cake for a richer effect.

## TRIANGULAR TOP

**1** Spread one layer of a Victoria sponge cake with buttercream and pipe two rows of shells around the edge. Cut the second cake in half horizontally and use the bottom piece for other purposes. Dredge the top with confectioner's sugar, making a pattern through a doily. Cut it carefully into three. Position the pieces on top of the cake with a cake slice.

**2** Pipe lines of cream shells over the joints. Decorate the top with split almonds, angelica and a cherry in the center.

## SPLIT TOP DECORATION

**1** Spread one layer of a Victoria sponge cake with buttercream. Draw a line over the cream with a skewer to give the halfway mark. Pipe a double row of buttercream shells around half the cake edge, piping them more heavily on the center edges than at the sides. Do the same around the other half if you want to create a butterfly effect with the finished cake.

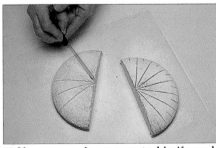

**2** Use a very sharp serrated knife and carefully slice the second cake in half horizontally. Dredge the top with confectioner's sugar and cut the cake in

half. Mark a decorative pattern in the confectioner's sugar with a skewer as shown.

**3** Being careful not to touch the top of the cake with your fingers, which would leave prints, place the two halves in position on top of the buttercream shells using a cake slice. One half should stand open resting on the buttercream shells or both if you have piped shells around both sides.

**4** Pipe a line of buttercream shells across the joint and decorate with cherries and angelica.

# DECORATING ROLLS

Cylindrical cakes can either be made with sponge cake batter and rolled up (see p. 20) or with fruit batter baked in a cylindrical pan.

### JELLY ROLL

**1** Cover the jelly roll with butter-cream, taking it down the sides. Leave the underside and the ends uncovered.

**2** Dip the sides of the cake in chocolate sprinkles and either pipe ridges along the top with a fine tip or mark ridges with a fork.

**3** Pipe a line of shells across the center of the cake and decorate it with walnuts, cherries and angelica.

*The ridges on this decorated jelly roll BELOW can either be piped or marked with a small fork.*

## YULE LOG

This traditional Yule log decoration makes a simple, but attractive Christmas cake.

**1** To make the ends of the log look like sawn wood, roll out a thin square of creamy yellow fondant icing and brush it with brown food color diluted in water. Cut the icing into strips. Join the strips up into a continuous length and roll the length up.

**2** With a very sharp knife, cut two thin slices off the roll Set the roll aside.

**3** Flatten the slices to merge the strips into one, and create a pattern of age rings as in the trunk of a tree. Cut the circles to size to fit the ends of the cake.

**4** Fix the circles to the ends of the cake with chocolate buttercream. Cover the sides of the cake with buttercream and run the back of a fork along the surface to create a bark effect.

**5** For the sawn-off branches, roll a fat sausage of brown marzipan about ¾ inch thick. Cut the ends off at 90 degrees to the roll and then cut it in two with a diagonal cut.

**6** Position the diagonal ends in the buttercream. Cut two small circles from the fondant icing roll to cover the ends of the branches. Cover the branches with buttercream and use the back of a fork to create bark as before.

**7** Finish the decoration with a robin and an axe and sprinkle the cake with sifted confectioner's sugar for a snowy effect.

# COATING AND PIPING WITH FONDANT

## COATING PETITS FOURS

To make simple fondant icing to cover petits fours, break down a European or Australian fondant (see pp. 40–41) with stock syrup (see p. 36).

Melt the fondant in a double boiler over hot water. Do not let the water boil or the shine will be lost from the cooled fondant. It may take 15 to 20 minutes to melt. Add enough stock syrup to make a soft flowing icing that will coat the back of a spoon. It is important not to stir the icing too vigorously, or you will incorporate air bubbles.

Petits fours can be cut from slabs of sponge cake to any shape. Popular shapes are diamonds, squares, circles and hearts. To ensure clear shapes, always wipe the knife or cutter to remove any traces of cake between each incision. Coat the petits fours with boiled apricot jam and, for a more professional finish, cover them with marzipan.

**1** Dip the cake into the fondant. The marzipan or apricot glaze will prevent crumbs getting into the fondant. Push the cake right down, so that the sides are evenly coated.

**2** Using a fork, and being careful not to put your fingers in the icing, lift the cake out of the fondant.

**3** Set it on a wire rack. The fondant will level itself out on the cake and any excess will drip off the bottom. You can scrape this up afterwards, warm it and use it again.

**4** Finish the cakes by setting them in paper cups when dry and piping a design on the top. You can also use fondant for piping (see overleaf), melted down and mixed with a little stock syrup to make it quite runny, with added coloring.

## COATING A ROUND CAKE

Prepare the cake by glazing with boiled apricot jam and/or coating with marzipan. Melt the fondant in a double boiler and add stock syrup to thin it down if necessary.

1 Stand the cake on a wire rack and pour the fondant carefully on to the centre of it. Give it a fairly thick coating so that it will run over the sides of the cake. The excess will drip through the mesh of the rack.

2 Use a metal spatula to smooth over the top and sides of the cake. Tap the wire rack a few times on the counter to settle the icing. As it settles, it will drip off the base. It is important to use a wire rack, so that the fondant does not build up at the bottom of the cake and spoil its shape.

## COATING A SQUARE CAKE

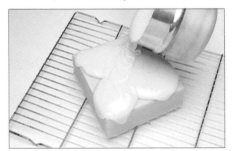

1 Prepare the fondant as for a round cake, and stand the square cake on a wire rack. Pour the fondant over the cake from corner to corner in a diagonal cross.

2 Use the metal spatula to push the fondant from the center of the cake to the sides and down the edges, working fairly fast before it starts to set. Tap the wire rack on the counter to settle the fondant and dislodge any air bubbles.

## PIPING WITH FONDANT

1 Add a little melted chocolate to some fairly runny fondant and pipe it straight from the pastry bag, cut off at the point to give a fine line. Some chandelier designs are shown in chocolate piping on page 80. Embroidery pattern books are a good source of ideas for attractive designs.

2 A more complicated design is piped on the round cake, using five colors of fondant. To stop the petals flowing into each other, pipe alternate petals and wait for them to set slightly before piping the petals in between.

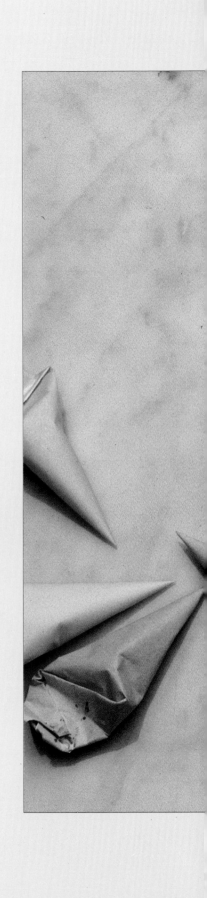

*Fondant is piped straight from the bag without a tip. It can be used to create fairly intricate effects as shown RIGHT.*

# MAKING DECORATIONS

Choosing and making decorations is an important part of cake decorating. Whether they are an integral part of the design or added at the last moment as a finishing touch, they must look right on the cake and not spoil the effect by being out of proportion or made from the wrong material.

This section demonstrates several different ways of making decorations, as well as showing how to paint decorations on cakes with food color and illustrating a selection of items from the bewildering range of ready-made edible and inedible decorations. Edible decorations can be made from marzipan, fondant icing, gelatin icing, modeling or petal paste, sugar and meringue mixes or chocolate. Different effects are achieved with each. Choose a material which you find easy to work with and which is appropriate to your cake. Some of the ideas for decorations included here are not used in any of the cake designs in Section 2. You may want to incorporate some of these into your own designs or you may like to make them as extra items for a festive occasion, for example, chocolate shapes to hang on the Christmas tree, marzipan rabbits for Easter Sunday or sugar mice for a children's party.

## EDIBLE DECORATIONS

The decorations illustrated here are all edible, and are just some of the enormous range of ready-made cake decorations available from both specialist and non-specialist sources.

1 *Sugar Christening cradle*
2 *Sugar stork*
3 *Sugar vase containing artificial heather sprays*
4 *Selection of corner leaves and decorations*
5 *Selection of zinnias*
6 *Multi-colored six-petal narcissi*
7 *Selection of wafer roses and leaves*
8 *Sugar pansies*
9 *Sugar violets*
10 *Assorted sugar flowers*
11 *Small sugar blossoms*
12 *Sugar 'stick-on' pre-formed flower candle holders*
13 *Sugar 'stick-on' pre-formed lettering*
14 *Selection of sugar novelties*

A selection of inedible cake decorations is illustrated here. The more conventional decorations for celebration cakes include wedding bells and horseshoes, keys for 18th and 21st birthdays, cupid for an engagement or valentine and a variety of flowers. For sporting birthday cakes, there are tennis rackets, golf clubs and footballers. For children, there are animals, robots and a toy train with a candle on each carriage. The rosette is made from a laced ribbon – when the laces are pulled, the ribbon loops up into the rosette shape.

The range is almost infinite. You can, after all, put anything you like on a cake.

# PAINTING WITH FOOD COLOR

There is a great variety of food coloring and cake decorating materials available on the market today, making it possible to achieve a wide range of decorative effects. The range of colors is constantly being extended, and the quality of colors improving. The most common method of coloring icing is to add it to the icing, and then apply the icing to the cake. Unfortunately, there are certain circumstances where this produces rather false colors. Leaf green, for example, when added to icing, never produces an authentic leaf color, no matter how much color is used. However, leaf green does produce a beautiful and authentic shade of green if the food color is used as a paint. In fact, by using the color in this way it is possible not only to

reproduce more subtle and true life shades, but also to achieve a greater variety of decorative effects.

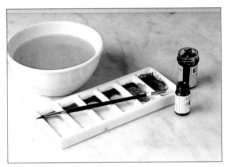

1 Food colors can be used like any watercolor paint. For example, adding water will make the color paler and mixing different colors can produce some interesting and exciting shades of color.

2 In order to make food colors fade into each other, apply the chosen colors to the surface being decorated so that they lie immediately next to each other. Whilst the colors are still wet make gentle brushstrokes across where the colors meet, merging one into the other.

*Food color comes in several different forms: as powder, paste, liquid and fiber-tip pens. Experiment with the different types until you find the one that suits you best. A couple of fine paintbrushes and a white saucer or an artist's plastic palette are the only other materials you will need.*

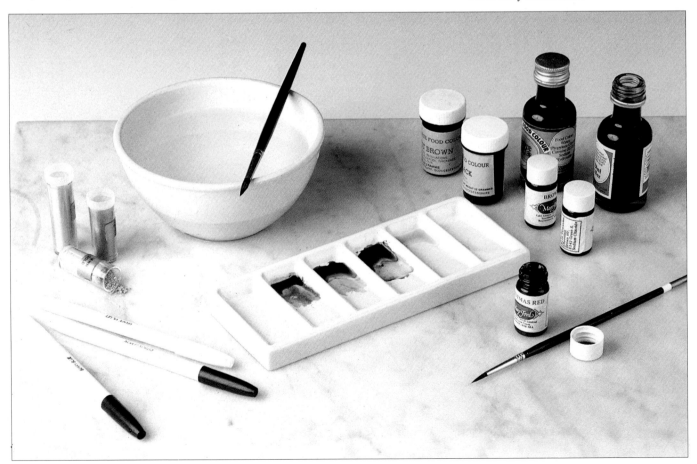

**3** To produce wood grain effect, mix the color required in a palette or saucer. Using a medium-sized paint-brush, dip the brush into the color shaking off any excess coloring. The brush should not be too wet. Press the brush down on to a work surface so that the bristles splay out into points. Gently brush across the surface of the icing to produce several lines.

often, you risk creating a streaked effect. Gently brush backwards and forwards until the surface is completely covered. Let the colors dry. Once dry it is possible to paint a design over the wash without disturbing the color background, as illustrated.

**6** To produce a stippled or marbled effect, mix the colors required and make sure the brush is not too wet. Press the brush down vertically on to a counter so that the bristles splay out into a rough circle of points. Lift the brush and holding it vertically, lightly dot the surface of the icing, as illustrated. In all cases when color decorating, *practise* on a spare piece of icing before painting the design on to the cake.

**5** When painting certain details or designs on a cake, it might be helpful to have an outline drawn on the cake beforehand using either black food color or a food color pen. In either case be sure to let the outline dry completely before filling in the colors, as illustrated.

**4** To produce a color wash effect, make sure that the brush is full of color. If you have to dip the brush too

*If you are painting two different colors directly beside each other or one color over the top of another as BELOW, let the first color dry completely before applying the second. Otherwise the colors will bleed into each other.*

# MARZIPAN ANIMALS

Marzipan animals make delightful decorations for children's birthday cakes. The basic ideas demonstrated here can easily be adapted to other animals and figures.

Recipes for Marzipan are given on pp. 26-28. You will need a variety of modeling tools and kitchen equipment.

## RABBIT

1 Take a piece of white marzipan the size of an egg and roll out a cone for the rabbit's body. Make an indentation where the tail will fit. Make indentations at the larger end of the cone for the haunches. Roll a small ball of marzipan for the head.

2 Make an indentation with your little finger across the head, and roll it into a dumb bell shape.

3 Cut down the length of the thinner end to form the ears. Use the dog bone tool to make indentations in the ears, which you can line with pink marzipan if you wish.

4 Indent little holes for the eyes and nose. Fill in the eyes with white royal icing and add a cone of pink marzipan for the nose. Paint black dots for the eyeballs. Try to suggest that the rabbit is looking slightly to one side. With the 'U' tool, indent a smiling mouth.

5 Make a little carrot out of orange and green marzipan. Divide the pointed end of the cone to make the front legs, slightly open them out and fix the carrot between them. Adhere the head to the body with egg white, royal icing or melted chocolate.

## SCOTTIE DOG

1 Roll a sausage of dark brown marzipan about 4 inches long and ¾ inch thick. Cut off a quarter for the head and mark the remaining piece to divide it into three.

2 Snip a piece from the top of the rolled marzipan and lift it gently to form the tail. Cut through the sausage from beneath the tail to the end to make the back legs. The front legs are formed in the same way.

3 Twist the legs apart gently and arch the marzipan to form the dog's body. Adjust the legs so that the dog stands firmly. Mark its paws.

4 Take the head and pinch up two ears with your thumb and forefinger. Indent the ears with the dog bone tool.

5 Pull out the dog's whiskers by stroking with the thumb and forefinger, and snip it into a fringe with the scissors.

6 Press a small ball of pink marzipan between the whiskers with the 'U' tool to form the mouth, and add a red tongue. Make a depression for the nose with tool No. 5 and insert a small cone of black marzipan.

7 Make two indentations for the eyes and fill them with white royal icing. Paint on black dots to complete the eyes.

8 Position the head on the body at an angle and fix it in place. The tam o' shanter cap is made by rolling red and green marzipan together and pressing a red pompom on top. Complete the model by giving the dog a bone.

## GOLDFISH

1 Roll out a sausage of orange marzipan 1 inch thick and 2½ inches long. Make two indentations, one with the little finger very close to one end to form the mouth and the second with the index finger a little further from the other end to form the goldfish's tail.

2 Stroke the marzipan between the thumb and forefinger to form a fin on the top of the fish and press and flatten the other end to form the tail. Turn the tail slightly to one side so that the fish will stay upright. Use the dog bone tool to impress the mouth and make two holes for the eyes with tool No. 5.

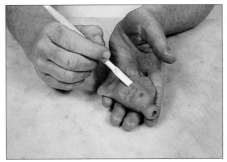

3 With shell tool No 2, mark the wavy lines on the fins, and use tool No. 4 to mark the scales.

4 Make the side fins by molding small cones of marzipan and flattening and curling them into shape. Adhere them to the sides of the fish with beaten egg white. Pipe royal icing for the eyes into the sockets. When the icing is dry, paint black dots to complete the eyes.

## DUCK

1 Roll four balls of white marzipan, one 2 inches across for the body, one 1½ inches across for the head, and two ½ inch across for the wings. Roll two balls of orange marzipan, one 1½ inches across for the feet and one ¼ inch across for the beak. Form the large white ball into a cone and drag the tip end of the cone across the work surface to form the uptilted tail. Squeeze the medium-sized white ball gently.

2 Flatten the two smallest white balls into teardrop shapes for the wings. Mark in feathers from the shoulder to the tip with shell tool No. 2. Feather-mark the tail in the same way. Elongate the larger orange ball for the feet by forming a depression across the center.

3 Press out the end of the dumb bell with your thumbs to make the feet. Mark the webs with shell tool No. 2. Roll the other orange ball into a cigar shape and fold in half to form the beak. Pinch the beak up in the middle so that it forms an open 'V' shape.

4 Assemble the duck. Adhere the body to the feet with lightly beaten egg white or melted chocolate. Position the beak on the body of the duck and press

the head on top, sandwiching the beak between the head and body. Attach the wings with lightly beaten egg white and pipe in the eyes with white royal icing. Mark the eyeballs and eyebrows. Add character with a little hat and by making a simple umbrella from a cone of marzipan and slipping it between a wing and the body.

## FROG

1 Form a ball of green marzipan 2 inches across into a pear shape and flatten and bend it over slightly at the top. Slice through the narrowest part with a sharp knife to form the mouth. Taking about half as much marzipan again, roll a dumb bell shape with one end larger than the other (as with the rabbit opposite). Roll two smaller balls for the protruding eye sockets.

2 Cut the dumb bell shape in half along its length to make the frog's legs. Twist the smaller end outward to form the foot and mark the webbed feet with tool No. 4.

3 Attach the legs and eye sockets to the body and make indentations for the eyeballs. Pipe in the eyeballs with white royal icing and complete the eyes with dots of black. Add three small balls
*continued overleaf*

# MARZIPAN FRUITS

of green marzipan to each foot for the toes. Make a few small holes in the frog's back and fill with orange marzipan to make spots. Give the frog a red tongue and adhere a tiny marzipan butterfly to the end of it.

## PIG

**1** Take a fat cone of pink marzipan and drag the pointed end across the counter to form an uptilted snout. With the blunt knife blade, tool No. 2, make a deep 'V' on the snout for the mouth and then make two indentations above the 'V' with the dog bone or ball tool for the nostrils. Make two more indentations for the eyes and ears to fit into and one more indentation at the back for the tail. Have ready four small pink balls for the legs, two cigar shapes for the ears and a long thin sausage for the tail.

**2** Push the slightly fatter end of the marzipan into the pig and twist it round to form a curly tail.

**3** Fill in the eyes with royal icing and dot them black. Flatten the ears between finger and thumb, adhere them in the indentations and flop them forward to give the pig character.

**4** Sit the body on top of the legs. For a finishing touch, add a hat (as with the snowman on page 68) or a bonnet cut from a flower shape.

You can either make marzipan fruits from different colored marzipan or use uncolored marzipan and paint them afterwards. A combination of both techniques gives delicate shading and a greater degree of realism.

For most of these fruits, start with a ball of marzipan about the size of a walnut. You will need a variety of modeling tools (pages 84-85), but you can improvise with kitchen equipment.

## LEMON

**1** Roll a ball of yellow marzipan, squeezing to give it two slightly pointed ends. Using a ball tool, indent the stalk end.

**2** Using the serrated end of modeling tool No. 4, work it over the fruit to give the appearance of lemon peel. Alternatively roll the marzipan lemon around on a nutmeg grater.

## PEAR

**1** Roll out a ball of yellow or green paste. Elongate the ball by rolling one side of it with your finger to form the neck of the pear. Roll your little finger around the base of the neck to form its 'waist'.

**2** Use the star tool to form the little indentations at the base and stalk of the pear. You can speckle it with brown marzipan to make it look more authentic.

## BANANA

Roll a piece of yellow marzipan into a sausage shape. Curve it with your fingers and flatten the sides to give it a banana shape. Paint or dust on strands of brown food color to give it a ripe appearance.

## APPLE, PLUM, APRICOT, CHERRY

For an apple, take red or green marzipan and roll it into a ball. Indent the top and tail with tool No. 5. Using appropriate colors make the other fruits in the same way. Use tool No. 2 to give an authentic crease to the fruit. Attach stamens to the cherries to represent stalks.

## STRAWBERRY

**1** Roll a red ball into a cone shape. Take a 4 inch square of fine tulle. Place the strawberry in the centre of the tulle.

**2** Draw the tulle up tightly around the marzipan and the fabric pattern will give a strawberry effect. Add a green paste leaf or a plastic culotte if available.

## ORANGE

Roll a ball of orange marzipan and use the serrated end of modeling tool No. 4 or a nutmeg grater to give the effect of peel. Use star tool No. 5 to make an indentation for the stem.

## GRAPES

For a bunch of grapes, roll a cone of purple or green paste and make several tiny balls to represent the grapes. Arrange the grapes all over the cone to form a bunch, pressing each one gently into position.

## FINISHING TOUCHES

**1** To finish your fruits, you can dust them with various colors for shading, give them a shine with gum arabic or coat them in sugar.

**2** To coat them in sugar, brush a little lightly beaten egg white on to the palm of your hand and roll the fruit in it. This is quicker than painting the fruit and you will get a lighter coat. Roll the fruit in superfine sugar to create a very pretty effect.

**3** Finally you can use chocolate sprinkles as miniature stems for the fruit. Alternatively, use cloves, but they may be too large. For the orange and the lemon, tiny star shaped soup noodles can be soaked for a second or two in a weak solution of green food coloring. If you allow them to soak longer, they will swell.

*A variety of fruits grouped together makes an attractive decoration for a plain cake.*

# MARZIPAN CHRISTMAS DECORATIONS

These brightly colored and festive decorations are great fun to make. When you are working with marzipan, keep two cloths handy, one damp and one dry, for cleaning your hands and tools. They get very sticky because of the almond oil. These decorations can also be made from fondant icing.

## CHRISTMAS TREE

**1** Form a cone of green marzipan. Take a very sharp pair of embroidery scissors and, starting at the top of the cone, snip small 'V' shapes into the marzipan to form branches.

**2** Lift each 'V' slightly as you withdraw the scissors to make the branches stand out. Continue snipping all round the tree until it is full of branches. You can use the same technique to make marzipan hedgehogs.

**3** Let the tree dry out thoroughly, then give it a seasonal touch of snow by sifting a little confectioner's sugar over the branches.

## HOLLY

**1** Roll out a sheet of green marzipan on a smooth counter lightly dusted with confectioner's sugar. Use a holly cutter if you have one or make a template from the illustration and cut round it with a fine sharp knife.

**2** Alternatively, use a small circular cutter, such as the end of a piping tip, and cut a series of circles in an oval shape, the sides of each circle touching the next to form the indentation of the leaf.

**3** As you cut the leaves, lay them on a piece of foam rubber and score the center of each leaf with a wooden pick to form a vein. At the same time this will make the leaves curl up at the sides. Make clusters of berries from small balls of red marzipan.

## SNOWMAN

**1** Make a cone of marzipan or, for a true white snowman, fondant icing. With tool No. 2, the blunt knife, make two upward cuts for arms and lever them out slightly to stand away from the body.

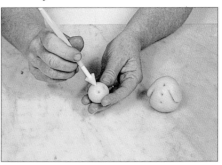

**2** Make a ball for the head and make indentations with star tool No. 5 where the eyes, nose and buttons are to be positioned.

**3** Push tiny cones of black marzipan into the holes for the eyes and buttons. A very small carrot cone shape makes the nose. A marzipan curl forms the mouth.

**4** The scarf is made from a long sausage of marzipan with the ends flattened and snipped to make a fringe. Make the hat by rolling a sausage of marzipan. Cut the ends flat. Make the hat brim by flattening out a little marzipan at the base of the hat between finger and thumb. Make some snowballs and set them beside the finished snowman.

## SANTA CLAUS

**1** The Santa Claus is rather more complicated and needs overnight drying before assembly. First roll a 4-inch sausage about ½ inch thick of red marzipan under the palm of your hand. Do not use your fingers because they will leave indentations on the sausage.

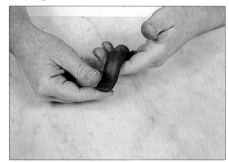

**2** Flatten the ends of the sausage and turn them up to form feet. Bow the sausage for the legs. Stand the legs up and let them dry.

**3** Make a cone for the body, indenting the base of the cone where the legs will be filled in.

**4** Make the arms from a 4-inch sausage about ¼ inch thick and at both ends cut the thumbs with tool No. 2. Smooth them off. Indent the palms with tool No. 2.

**5** Roll two equal-sized balls of marzipan for the head, one flesh colored and one red. Cut each of them in half and sandwich a red one for the hat on to a pink one for the face. You will not need the spare halves.

**6** Make a groove for the brow with tool No. 2. Make two indentations for the eye sockets. Use two tiny flattened balls of black marzipan for the eyes.

**7** Cut out the trimmings – the belt, beard, eyebrows and fur – with a knife. Stick the trimmings to the head, body, arms and legs with lightly beaten egg white. Let all the pieces dry.

**8** The next day, assemble the body by threading the legs, body and head on to a wooden pick or piece of uncooked spaghetti. Make a sackful of presents for the finishing touch.

*The complete Christmas decorations will appeal particularly to children.*

# MOLDED ROSES

Making a molded rose requires patience and a steady hand. The rose shown below is made with fondant icing. You can also use marzipan, though its slightly grainier texture means that the petals are less fine.

Molding fine shapes like petals with fondant icing or marzipan can be a problem if your hands and fingers get hot, because the fondant or marzipan will stick to them. There are two ways of preventing this. Either dust your fingers very lightly with cornstarch, or mold the petals inside a plastic bag. If you use the cornstarch method, make sure you use only a very little or it will spoil the look of the petals.

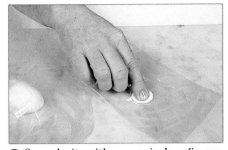

**3** Squash it with your index finger. Using both index fingers, flatten the paste at the top edge to form the edge of the petal. The base of the petal should remain thick so that it can be attached to the flower. Another way to mold the petals, if you have cool hands, is to stroke and pull the edge of the petal between your fingers, or to lay the petal on the palm of one hand and flatten and thin it with a ball tool.

**4** Wrap the first petal right around the cone with the top of the petal ¼ inch above the top of the cone. You should not need water to adhere the petals to the cone.

**5** Gently squeeze it in with your fingers to form a 'waist' at the bottom of the petal. The first petal should be completely closed around the cone.

**1** Roll a ball of fondant icing the size of an egg in your hands. Rub it in the heels of your hands until it forms a cone about 2 inches high and put it point upwards on your counter.

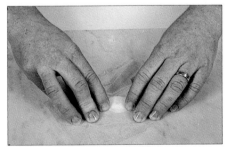

**2** To make each petal, follow the same technique. Roll a ball of fondant about the size of a large pea. Put it in a plastic bag or under a sheet of plastic.

**6** Place the center edge of the second petal opposite the joint line of the first petal and ¼ inch above it. Attach one side of the petal firmly to the cone and leave the other side free. Curl the tips of the petal back – do not wait too

long to do this or the fondant will dry and crack.

**7** Place the center of the third petal over the closed side of the second petal. Attach it on both sides of the cone and curl the tip back.

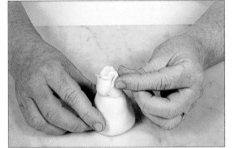

**8** Place the center of the fourth petal over the edge of the third and under the open side of the second. Close the edge of the second petal down. Curl the edge of the fourth petal back.

**9** With four petals pinched in neatly at the base, the three outer ones curled back at the tips, you have formed a rosebud. If you wish to stop at this stage, look at the flower from all angles, decide which is the best, and cut the bud from the cone at a slant, so that it will rest on the cake with the best side up.

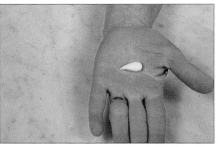

**10** To make a bigger rose, continue to build up the flower with slightly larger petals. It does not matter where you start attaching the outer petals. Stretch the base of each petal round as you secure it to the cone. Apply each petal so that it overlaps the previous one about halfway and curl the tips outwards.

**12** Turn the rose, gently pressing down each of the petals to ensure they are secured firmly at the base.

**14** To make a very small bud, roll a tiny cone shape on your palm into a rosebud shape.

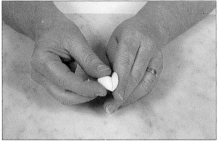

**11** Continue adding petals until the rose is fairly even and you have an attractive flower.

**13** Cut the base of the rose so that it will stand upright on the cake. Angle the base of each rose carefully according to its position in the final arrangement.

**15** Make one petal, wrap it round the cone and pinch it at the base to form a bud.

*These very attractive molded roses are used in the decoration of the Golden Wedding cake on p. 168.*

# PASTILLAGE

Pastillage work can be done with modeling paste, petal paste or gelatin icing. All three are equally suitable for molding flowers, figures and other decorations and the one you choose depends on the time and ingredients available. A recipe for gelatin icing is given on p. 35.

## MODELING PASTE

This recipe for pastillage includes confectioner's sugar, edible gums and other edible materials which impart flexibility and elasticity to the paste. Gum tragacanth is available from specialist cake decorating sources.

### INGREDIENTS
2 tsp gelatin
5 tsp cold water
1 lb confectioner's sugar, sifted
1 tbsp gum tragacanth
2 tsp light corn syrup
2 tsp white vegetable shortening
1 egg white

1 Soak the gelatin in the cold water for about half an hour. Meanwhile, heat the confectioner's sugar and gum tragacanth in a bowl over a pan of warm water.

2 Add the corn syrup and shortening to the gelatin and dissolve over very low heat.

3 Beat the sugar mixture in an electric mixer at a slow speed. Add the corn syrup mixture and the egg white. Turn the machine to maximum speed and beat for about 15 minutes. The longer and harder you beat the paste, the whiter it will be.

## PETAL PASTE

Petal paste is made simply by adding water to a special gum powder available from specialist cake decorating sources.

### INGREDIENTS
1½ tbsp water
2¾ cups petal paste powder
½ tsp white vegetable shortening (optional)

1 Put the water into a bowl. Sift in most of the petal paste powder. Always use water and powder in the ratio of 1:10.

2 Sift the remaining powder on to the counter. Work the contents of the bowl into a thick paste, then cover the bowl and let stand for 5 minutes to allow the gum to activate. Scrape the contents of the bowl out on to the counter.

3 Knead the paste until the rest of the powder is incorporated. This creates a smooth pliable paste. For greater elasticity, knead the white vegetable shortening into the paste.

4 The paste may be used immediately, but it is best left for 24 hours. Store the paste in an airtight container.

## MOLDED FLOWERS

This section shows you how to make a spray of tiny flowers, a larger single flower, a briar rose and an azalea. You could make all these flowers with fondant icing or marzipan, but as these tend to spoil in damp or humid conditions, it is better to use pastillage, following either of the recipes opposite.

Remember when you are working with the petals not to let them dry out completely before you finish molding and shaping, or they will break as you try to put the flower together.

Egg white and water can both be used to fix petals into position on the flower. Egg white forms a stronger bond, but in most cases, water should be sufficient. If the petals are left to dry, or should break off and need replacing, then they must be attached with royal icing. Be very careful not to paint any egg white on to any part of the flower that will show, because it will dry shiny. If you make any mistakes with water, they will not be visible.

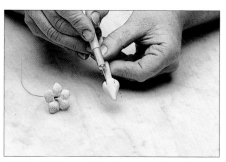

2 Push the point of a wooden skewer up into the wide base of the cone. Using a fine sharp knife, cut five even petals around the base of the cone, turning the skewer as you work.

3 Take out the skewer and turn the flower out into your fingers, in order to pull out the petals. Flatten each petal between thumb and forefinger and pull from underneath with your finger against your thumb, flattening and broadening the petal at the same time.

4 For the stalk, make a small hook at the end of a piece of covered wire, dampen the hooked end in water or beaten egg white and pull it through the center of the flower, hooking into the side of the flower.

5 Cut the stamen in half, dampen the cut ends, and push them into the center of the soft paste. As it hardens, it will hold them in position. Let dry in an upright position.

6 The result is a perfect flower that you can dust or paint to whatever shade you want.

## SINGLE BLOOM

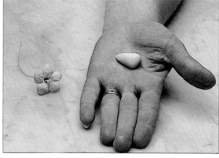

1 Form a cone of petal paste approximately ¾ inch long and ½ inch across the base.

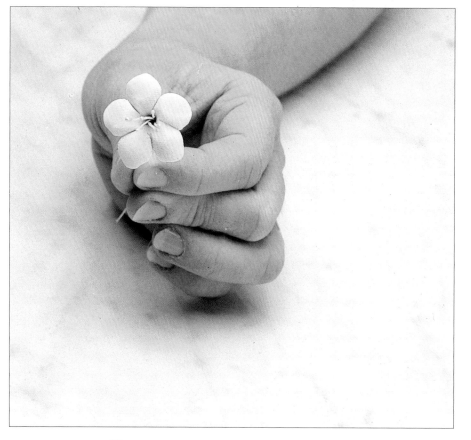

## BRIAR ROSE

**1** To make a briar or Christmas rose, you will need a shallow curved container to set the flowers in. Bottle tops, a paint palette (as here) or polystyrene fruit trays from the supermarket are all ideal.

To make the calyxes, color a little petal paste green. Cut out the shapes with a calyx cutter – or you can make your own with a template. Put the template on the petal paste and cut round it with a fine sharp knife. Line the base of each container with a small square of wax paper to prevent the petal paste from sticking and lay the calyxes on top. The calyx will curve to the shape of the container you put it in.

**2** Cut five small circles for petals from pink petal paste using a plain round cutter ¾ inch in diameter and lay them on foam rubber. Curl the petals with a modeling tool, such as the dog bone, by running it gently along the edge of the petal, half on the petal and half on the foam. A delicately frilled edge will result. To curve the petal, indent the base with the ball tool or your little finger, by pushing down into the foam rubber. Pull the end of the petal out to elongate it slightly.

**3** Paint inside the calyx with water or lightly beaten egg white and position the first petal carefully.

**4** Brush one side of the petal lightly with lightly beaten egg white or water and leave the other side free (the fifth petal will be tucked underneath it). Lay the second petal in place overlapping the painted edge and continue until four petals are in position. Slip the fifth petal in under the edge of the first. Paint the underside of the first to secure them in place.

**5** To make the center of the flower, roll a very small ball of yellow paste and press it into a fine piece of tulle, so that the weave of the fabric is imprinted on the paste, giving the effect of stamens. This technique can also be used in making a daisy. Position in the center of the flower and adhere with beaten egg white or water.

**6** Cut a few stamens about ¼ inch long and insert them into the center of the flower with a pair of tweezers.

*The end result is a very authentic-looking briar rose. Briar roses make very attractive decorations for royal-iced celebration cakes.*

## AZALEA

**1** To make an azalea you need a piece of doweling or a similar prop to fold the petals against. With a teardrop shaped cutter, or with a template, cut out five petals from the paste. Cover the petals you are not working on with plastic. Gently mark the center vein of the petal with a wooden pick and two on either side. Be careful not to press too heavily or you will slice through the petal. These marks will not really show until you come to color the flower.

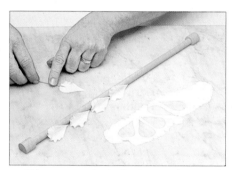

**2** To create a frilled edge to the petal, roll the wooden pick along the edge of the paste, thinning it to ¼ inch. Dust the counter with confectioner's sugar or cornstarch. Roll the petal with the left index finger. Line up each petal as it is finished against the doweling to curve it.

**3** To set the petals into a flower shape you will need a small cone – a little medicine funnel from a drugstore is ideal. Line it with wax paper or foil to stop the flower from sticking in the funnel. Drop the first petal into the funnel, paint half the length of one side with lightly beaten egg white or water and put the next petal in position overlapping the painted edge.

**4** To secure the petals in position press them gently together with the handle of the paintbrush. Continue until you have four petals in position. The fifth petal will form the azalea's tongue. Nick off the point and drop it in over the first and fourth petals.

**5** Pipe a tiny spot of royal icing from a bag into the throat of the flower and, with a pair of tweezers, insert seven stamens, six of equal length and one longer for the pistil. Leave the flower to dry. Once the flower is completely dry, you can paint it with food colors or dust it with petal dust, which is a dry powder applied with a broad soft brush. Put a little cotton into the cup of the flower so that the petal dust touches only the edges. Brush from the outside inwards to get a graduated effect. Paint little spots on the tongue of the azalea by dampening a fine brush in water and then in the petal dust.

*The petal dust gives the finished azaleas a sheen. Azaleas are used in the Hexagonal Wedding Cake on p. 160.*

## FLOWER SPRAYS

**1** It is important to roll out pastillage as thinly as possible. Put a piece of paste the size of a large pea on a smooth counter that you have lightly dusted with confectioner's sugar or cornstarch or a mixture of both. Remember that cornstarch is a drying agent, so use it very sparingly. Use either a stainless steel rolling pin or a short length of smooth wooden doweling.

Each time the paste is rolled, lift the paste with a metal spatula to ensure that it does not stick to the counter. Roll the paste out so that it is thin enough to read through when you lay it on a printed page.

**2** Plunger cutters are very useful gadgets for making petal paste flowers. Press the cutter into the paste and give it a gentle twist.

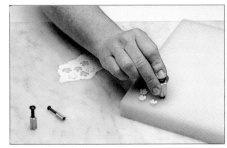

**3** Lift the cutter together with the cut flower and, holding the cutter on a piece of foam rubber, depress the plunger. As it is pushed into the foam, the paste will be cupped and will form the shape of a flower. You can use a cutter without a plunger, in which case push the flower out of the cutter with a paintbrush.

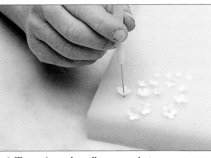

**4** To wire the flowers into a spray, prick a hole in the center of each one with a thick needle. Do this before they have dried or they will break.

**5** Stamens come with a knob at each end, so cut them in half and double the number. To insert a stamen, put it into the hole in the flower and pull it halfway through. Letting the flower rest on your fingertips, squeeze a little royal icing from a bag (you do not need a tip) into the base of the flower and pull the stamen gently down into it. Turn the flowers upside down to dry.

**6** To make a bud using a stamen as its base, take a tiny amount of paste, flatten it between finger and thumb and roll it up round the stamen. Dampen the tip of the stamen in lightly beaten egg white or water first so that the paste will stick.

**7** To attach flowers and buds to a spray, use white floristry tape. Take a 4-inch strip and cut it in half

widthways. Stretch it out until it is about four times its original length.

**8** Lay the tape along your index finger and roll the wire stalk into the tape. Start arranging your spray. Put one or two buds at the top of the wire, catching the last ¼ inch of the stamen bases in the tape with the wire as you turn it.

**9** Start adding the flowers one by one and, as you roll the tape around the stalk, catching the base of the stamens, the tape will travel down the wire so that each flower is slightly lower than the preceding one.

**10** Use five to seven flowers to a spray. Finish by completely covering the wire with the tape, then cut the stalk off to a length of about 2 inches. Flower sprays are used on several of the cakes in Section 2, including the Christening Cake, Engagement Cake and the Hexagonal Wedding Cake.

## RIBBON LOOPS

Ribbon loops are usually used in sprays of about 12 to 16 and each will take about 12-18 inches of ribbon. They are a very useful decoration for celebration cakes.

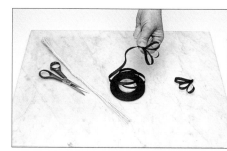

**1** To make ribbon loops, you need ¼ inch ribbon, a sharp pair of scissors and some fine covered wire. Make three equal sized loops and cut off the remaining ribbon.

**2** With the loops in your palm and the ends of the ribbon held between thumb and forefinger, place the covered wire under the ribbon ends. Turn the ends of the ribbon over the wire parallel to the sides of the ribbon. Twist the wire into the center of the ribbon loop and wind it tightly together to cover all the ends. Cut the wire about ¼ inch from the ends of the ribbon.

**3** To decorate a cake, place the ends of the wire into a ball of fondant which has been put in position on the cake.

**4** Place the first loop into the center of the ball of fondant with the ribbon ends facing out from the center of the cake. Place another ribbon loop directly opposite, again with the ribbon ends pointing down and out from the center. In order to form a cross, place two more loops at 90 degrees and then fill in with more loops. If necessary go round again filling in between loops with another row of loops. Colors may be alternated.

*Ribbon loops are used interwined with flower sprays BELOW to make a central decoration for the Golden Wedding Cake (see p. 168).*

# SUGAR & CHOCOLATE DECORATIONS

## SUGAR BELLS

**1** To make these attractive wedding decorations, you will need bell molds of different sizes, superfine sugar and lightly beaten egg white or water. Mix the sugar with the egg white or water until it has a coarse, thick consistency. Pack the mixture solidly into the molds, which should be perfectly clean, and scrape the base with a knife to make it completely flat.

**2** Hold the mold upside down over a sheet of paper and gently tap out the bell. It should come out quite cleanly. Make sure the mold is completely clean and dry before re-use.

**3** Leave the bells until they are dry to the touch. If they become too hard, they will break when you try to hollow out the centers.

**4** Pick the bell up gently, or slip it back into the mold if you are afraid of breaking it, and carefully scrape out the center with a sharp knife. Use the scrapings to make more bells or sugar mice. Either make a hollow just in the center or scrape out the bell until it is a delicate ¾ inch thick.

## SUGAR MICE

**1** To make sugar mice, mix superfine sugar with lightly beaten egg white or water as for the sugar bells. Leave half the mixture white and color the other half pink and pack solidly into the molds. Turn the mice out on to wax paper.

**2** Make their tails with pieces of string, thin sausages of fondant icing or pipe them with royal icing. Pipe pink eyes and noses for the white mice and chocolate features for the pink mice. The same molds can also be used for marzipan, chocolate or fondant mice.

## MERINGUE MUSHROOMS

**1** First make a meringue mixture and, using tip No. 3 or 4, pipe the stems of the mushrooms, bringing them up to a point. Make them flat at the bottom, so that they do not topple over when assembled. Pipe little beads or circles for the caps of the mushrooms. Pull the tip gently to the side to remove it, instead of pulling it up, or it will make a point. If you do get a point, however, push it down with a dampened finger and it will disappear.

**2** Sprinkle the mushroom tops with sifted cocoa and bake on a cookie sheet covered with wax paper in a very cool oven for an hour or two. To test if they are done, tap them lightly with your finger. They should sound hollow and lift easily off the paper.

**3** To assemble the mushrooms, make a tiny hollow under the cap with your little finger or a ball tool. Push the stem into the cap and stand them up.

## LEAVES

**1** Cut a paper pattern for the leaf shape you require. Pin it to a piece of green tulle and cut round the tulle to the shape of your pattern.

**2** Place the tulle leaf on a strip of wax paper and pipe round the edge with green royal icing. A delicate scalloped edge is shown, but you can pipe a shell border or a snail trail – as long as it hides the cut edge of the leaf.

**3** Pipe the center vein and the smaller veins at the side with pale green royal icing and a fine tip.

**4** If you want to make the leaf curl, secure a rolling pin to the counter by placing a small ball of icing under each end. Before the leaf dries, curl it on its wax paper round the rolling pin. Stick the paper to the rolling pin with two dabs of icing. You can make all kinds of leaves in this way, to use among floral decorations.

## CRYSTALLIZED FLOWERS

Crystallized flowers make spectacular decorations for a cake or gâteau.

Choose only the very best specimens for decoration. Paint the petals, the leaves or the whole flower with gum arabic, then dip in superfine sugar. Let dry overnight on a wire rack.

## FROSTED FRUIT

Choose top quality soft fruit, such as strawberries, grapes or mandarin orange slices. Paint with lightly beaten egg white, dip in superfine sugar and use as a center decoration for the dinner table or serve after dinner with coffee.

## EASTER EGGS

**1** To make these miniature Easter egg decorations, make sure the mold is perfectly clean.

**2** Make sure that the chocolate is not too hot (see p. 80), then pour it – either from a spoon or a saucepan – into the mold. Fill the mold all the way to the edge.

**3** Leave the mold until the eggs are ready to be released. As the chocolate begins to release from the mold by itself, it will turn slightly opaque. Turn the mold upside down and the eggs will fall out.

**4** Let the eggs dry completely, then cover them with different colors of royal icing.

*When the chocolate Easter eggs are dry, decorations can be piped on them with colored icing and a very fine tip.*

# CHOCOLATE DECORATIONS

You can use baking chocolate or ordinary eating chocolate for many different kinds of decoration. The chocolate is first melted, then either poured out to make a sheet, from which the shapes are cut, or piped.

When melting chocolate it is important not to let it get too hot or it will get too runny. Break the chocolate into pieces and put it in a double boiler. Do not allow the water to boil. The chocolate should never be above body temperature or the oil will separate out of it and it will become unusable. A quick way to test for temperature without a thermometer is to dab your finger in the chocolate and touch it to your lip. It should feel neither hot nor cold. It may take up to half an hour to melt chocolate in this way, but the results will be well worth the extra time.

Remember that if you handle chocolate, the warmth of your fingers will leave prints on it and dull the surface. Handle it as little as possible, preferably using a metal spatula.

## CHOCOLATE FOR CUTTING

**1** When the chocolate has melted pour it out on to a sheet of parchment paper. This is release paper, so the shapes will come away easily.

**2** Lift the edges of the paper and tilt the chocolate in different directions to ensure the surface is smooth and even after pouring. Leave it to stand until almost rubbery, but not hard, before you cut the shapes.

## SQUARES AND DIAMONDS

With a sharp knife, cut parallel lines across the chocolate. Cut another set of equidistant parallel lines at 90 degrees to make squares. Cut the second set of parallel lines at 45 degrees for diamonds. Use a ruler or cut freehand.

## CIRCLES

Cut circles by pressing in and giving a slight twist with a round cutter. Make rings by cutting a smaller circle inside the first circle. You can leave the shapes in the sheet of chocolate or put them on one side to dry.

## HORSESHOES, HEARTS AND STARS

Horseshoes, hearts and stars are all cut in the same way as circles. Cut small holes in your shapes with a tiny round cutter and thread ribbon through them when dry to hang on the Christmas tree or give as gifts. Hearts dressed with ribbon make attractive valentines.

## CURLS

Make long chocolate curls by pushing a smoother or plain icing comb down the length of the sheet of chocolate. This lifts a thin layer off the surface and the chocolate will curl up. Cut it into strips to decorate cakes or make bark for a forest scene.

## LEAVES

One way to make chocolate leaves is paint the back of a leaf with melted chocolate and peel off the leaf when it has dried. Alternatively, pipe a leaf shape using melted chocolate and draw on the veins with a wooden pick after it has set slightly.

## PIPING WITH CHOCOLATE

**1** You can pipe an infinite number of attractive decorations to use on cakes and ice-cream with melted chocolate. Work quickly because the chocolate starts to set rapidly. With a fleurs-de-lis shape, wait for the first section to dry slightly before attempting the second, and so on, otherwise the shapes will run into each other. Chocolate buttons are fun to make and can be coated with chocolate sprinkles or tiny candies.

**2** More intricate shapes, such as flowers or chandeliers, can be outline-piped to give a good contrast with the cake topping, which will show through underneath. These can be piped as a continuous line, provided the chocolate is the right consistency. If it is too hot, the lines will flow together. If it is too cold, it will not come out of the pastry bag.

*Squares*

*Diamonds*

*Circles*

*Hearts and stars*

*Fleur-de-lis and other piped shapes*

*Curls*

*Leaves*

*Outline-piped shapes*

# ELABORATE DECORATING TECHNIQUES

Before attempting one of the elaborate royal- or fondant-iced cakes in Section Two, make sure you are familiar with the techniques demonstrated in this section. A useful way of practicing is to ice a polystyrene cake dummy and then try out the different piping techniques on it. This will help you choose your cake design, by giving you a chance to discover which types of decoration you like and find easy.

This section opens with the fundamentals – basic equipment and icing tips, covering with marzipan, royal and fondant icing and making a pastry bag. It then demonstrates a variety of piping techniques, making lace, run-outs, piping flowers and borders and finally making templates for positioning pillars on tiered cakes and assembling tiers.

## EQUIPMENT

The equipment illustrated opposite is a selection of items used in the decoration of elaborate royal- and fondant-iced celebration cakes.

1 *Heavy-duty icing turntable*
2 *Plaster wedding cake pillars*
3 *Plastic wedding cake pillars, with hollow centers for wooden skewers*
4 *Polystyrene cake dummy for practice and display purposes*
5 *Wooden skewers*
6 *A selection of shaped ½-inch cake boards and thin cake cards*

7 *Large flexible plastic icing smoother or plain icing comb for fondant icing*
8 *Small stainless steel scraper for royal icing*
9 *Small flexible plastic smoother or plain icing comb*
10 *Stainless steel straight edge for applying royal icing*
11 *Short spatula for general mixing and filling work*
12 *Handled smoother or icing comb for fondant icing an alternative to the large flexible smoother*
13 *Silver banding for cakes and cake boards*

Illustrated here is a selection of tools used in elaborate cake decoration

**1** *Thread-coated floristry wire*
**2** *Modeling tools (from left to right): paddle and U shape (No. 4); Shell and blade (No. 2); Cone and star tool (No. 5); Ball tool (No. 3); Dog bone shape (No. 1)*
**3** *Stainless steel scriber, for marking patterns on to icing*
**4** *Tip cleaning brush*
**5** *Fine-pointed tweezer*
**6** *Cranked handle metal spatula*
**7** *Set of crimpers*
**8** *Stainless steel rolling pin*
**9** *Selection of fine paintbrushes*
**10** *Selection of edible food color*
**11** *Strong paste food colors*
**12** *Dry color*
**13** *Frill or flounce cutter*
**14** *Flower cutters (top row from left to right); Briar rose; Serrated rose leaf; Blossom-shaped plunger cutters; (bottom row) Star or rose calyx cutters; Rose petal or azalea petal cutters*
**15** *Selection of 1/2 inch aspic cutters*
**16** *Flower nails*
**17** *Selection of graduated cookie cutters*
**18** *Hollow plastic bell-shaped molds*
**19** *Selection of number cutters*
**20** *Artificial stamens*

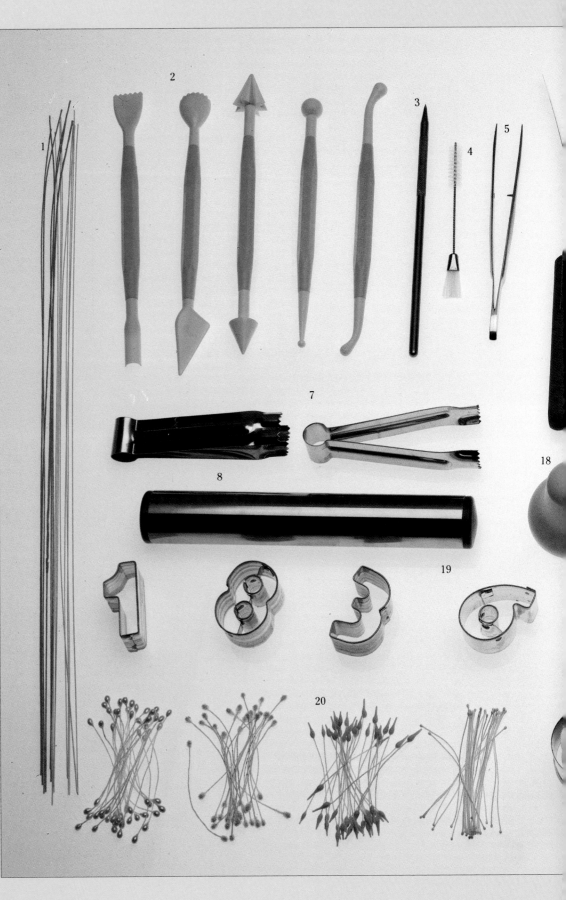

# ICING  TIPS

There are many different kinds of icing tips on the market. It is better to buy the more expensive tips because they have very finely cut edges, which give accurate shapes and are more durable. If you buy inexpensive tips and find that the edges are rather rough or banned, file them down with emery paper.

All  the shapes – star, shell, petal, basket weave, leaf and so on – come in varying widths. A full range comprises between 15 and 25 sizes.
To begin with you will need a fine

writing tip, which is round and also produces a beaded 'snail trail', a shell tip and perhaps a petal tip. With these three basic tools you can create a wide range of designs.

Icing tips should always be kept clean – even a fine obstruction, such as a hair, can spoil the regular outline of the shape you are trying to pipe. A special icing tip brush is available for cleaning tips.

Different manufacturers use different numbers to designate the widths of the

tips, but smaller numbers always refer to finer tips. The tips used in this book are made by Bekenal Products Ltd. (For Wilton tip equivalents, see page 194.)

It is possible to pipe without a tip straight from the bag (the leaves on the Valentine cake on p. 126 were made without tips and chocolate work is usually done without tips), but the addition of a few tips to your icing kit will give you greater scope and variety.

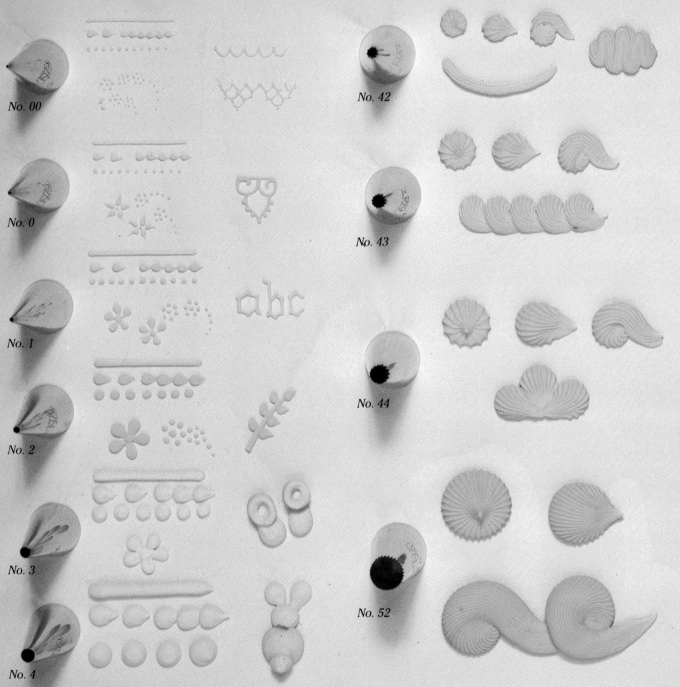

No. 00

No. 0

No. 1

No. 2

No. 3

No. 4

No. 42

No. 43

No. 44

No. 52

*No. 5*

*No. 7*

*No. 9*

*No. 11*

*No. 12*

*No. 13*

*No. 15*

*No. 57*

*No. 58*

*No. 59*

*No. 22*

*No. 37*

Nos. 00, 1, 2, 3 and 4 are plain tips used for lettering, straight lines, pearling, beading, lace and extension work. No. 00 is very fine and susceptible to blockages. No. 1 is particularly suitable for lettering. No. 2 is used for pressure piping – building up small icing figures – and trellis work – as well as the general uses. Nos. 3 and 4 are used for foundation lines for built-up work and piping strongly defined patterns on to large cakes.

Nos. 42, 43, 44 and 52 are rope tips with finely cut teeth which give a ribbed, ropelike texture to the surface of shells, beads, swirls and scrolls. No. 44 is particularly suitable for larger cakes, such as the lower tiers of a wedding cake. No. 52 is used for very large scrolls and curves. This tip requires a larger pastry bag.

Nos. 5, 7, 9, 11, 12, 13 and 15 are shell or star tips. No. 5 is mainly used for piping shell borders around the base of cakes and for overpiping scroll work. No. 9 has only six teeth, compared with eight on most of the other shell tips, and creates a slightly different effect. No. 11 is very useful for shells and scrolls on 10-inch and 12-inch cakes. No. 12 is useful for piping stars into which birthday cake candles can be set before the icing dries. No. 13 has twelve teeth and gives a finely ridged finish. No. 15 is the largest star tip and can be used for buttercream.

Nos. 57, 58 and 59 are petal tips with a crescent-shaped opening. Delicate petal shapes can be piped together to form simple flowers. No. 57 is suitable for piping violets, pansies and other small flowers. No. 59 can be used to create an attractive pleated ribbon effect.

No. 22 is used for piping a basket weave effect.

No. 37 can be used to make a simple flower with one squeeze of the pastry bag, or a braided effect by piping continuous, slightly uneven lines.

# COVERING WITH MARZIPAN

## FOR ROYAL ICING

A common problem with cakes covered in marzipan and then royal icing is that the icing becomes discolored by the marzipan beneath. This happens usually because there is too much oil in the marzipan and it has not been allowed to dry thoroughly before being covered with icing. Allow the cake plenty of time to dry and use a cooked, not uncooked, marzipan.

This problem does not occur with bought marzipan. If possible, choose white or naturally colored marzipan.

**1** Always turn the cake over to decorate it, so that the flat base becomes the top. What is now the base of the cake may be concave or convex and this should be dealt with. Either slice off the rounded part if it is concave or fill the hollow with marzipan if it is convex.

**2** Roll a long, thin sausage of marzipan and stick it round the base of the cake with jam or lightly beaten egg white by pressing it into the cake with a metal spatula. This will both seal the edges of the cake to the cake board and help the cake to keep longer.

**3** Sprinkle the counter with confectioner's sugar. Roll out the marzipan, using spacers as a guide to even thickness and the right width, which should be a little more than the diameter of the cake.

**4** Turn the marzipan over, sprinkling more confectioner's sugar beneath it if necessary. The smoother rolled side of the marzipan is the 'right' side. Brush a circle of warm apricot jam or lightly beaten egg white the same size as the diameter of the cake on the 'wrong' side of the marzipan. Alternatively, brush the cake with jam. Apricot is generally used rather than other jams because it does not dominate the flavor of the marzipan.

**5** Place the cake top down on the marzipan. Cut the marzipan closely round the cake.

**6** Turn the cake the right way up, being careful not to leave finger marks in the marzipan. Trim off any excess marzipan from the bottom sausage. Ensure that the sides of the cake are smooth, filling any small holes with pieces of marzipan.

**7** Roll out a strip of marzipan about ¼ inch thick for the sides of the cake. The length of the strip should be three times the diameter of the cake. Measure the depth of the strip to fit the sides. Make sure your counter is well dusted with confectioner's sugar. Turn the marzipan over, so that the smoother side is face down. Brush the marzipan with warm apricot jam or lightly beaten egg white.

**8** Roll the cake along the marzipan, pressing it into position. If you have miscalculated, and you need to add a little extra marzipan, it will not show if the joints are neat.

**9** If you are covering a square cake, measure the sides of the cake and cut two pieces to fit. Attach them to opposite sides of the cake and measure the two remaininig sides plus the thickness of the marzipan before cutting and fitting. This will give you 90-degree corners. Otherwise follow the instructions for the round cake.

**10** Now the cake is completely covered, smooth it carefully with the heel and palm of your hands. A smooth, flat coating of marzipan will provide the perfect base for a professional icing for the cake.

## FOR FONDANT ICING

If you intend to finish your cake with fondant rather than royal icing, a slightly different technique is involved. The marzipan needs to be rounded at the corners and edges, because the fondant is applied to the top and sides of the cake in one process. Use warm beaten apricot jam or lightly beaten egg white to hold the marzipan in position.

Fondant icing does not become discolored by marzipan in the way that royal icing does, so either natural or colored marzipan can be used.

**1** Turn the cake upside down, so that the flatter surface becomes the top. Trim the sides if necessary and fill any holes with marzipan dampened with lightly beaten egg white. Roll a long, thin sausage of marzipan for the base of the cake, paint the edge of the cake with lightly beaten egg white and attach the marzipan.

**2** Press the marzipan on to the cake with a metal spatula to secure it. Do not use your fingers.

**3** Turn the cake the right way up and place it on a sheet of wax paper. Moisten the cake all over with lightly beaten egg white.

**4** Roll out a square of marzipan large enough to cover the top and sides of the cake, allowing for some surplus.

**5** Pick up the marzipan right-side up. Use your right hand to pick up the marzipan and slide it over your left hand. Drape it over the cake.

**6** Hold the marzipan up from beneath with one hand and smooth it down with the other towards the raised hand to exclude air bubbles.

**7** Once the top is flat, flare out the corners. Make sure you do not stretch the marzipan too much, or it will crack and craze. Smooth and fit the corners using the palm of your hand before you fit the sides. Make sure the sides are flat and not pleated or creased.

**8** Use the warmth of your hand to help smooth off the marzipan and ensure it is well fixed to the cake.

**9** With a metal spatula trim the marzipan to the base of the cake making a neat edge all the way around.

# COVERING WITH ROYAL ICING

Leave the marzipan for two or three days for the surface to harden slightly before you ice the cake. If you are working in damp conditions, you may have to put the cake in a warm dry place for it to harden.

Make up the royal icing (see p. 38) with a sufficient quantity to give the cake three coats. Give the cake top a coat with the freshly made icing, which should be well aerated from beating. Always keep the bowl of icing covered as you work. Let the top dry for about six hours or overnight before you start to work on the sides. Do not try and hurry the drying process – if you dry it in a low oven the icing will discolor, and it may crack as the cake expands and contracts. Leave icing covered at room temperature, do not refrigerate.

In this instance only, it does not matter if air bubbles are present, as the first layer of icing serves to provide a foundation on which subsequent finishing coats are applied.

**2** With a paddling motion, spread the icing towards the sides of the cake. Turn the cake as you tilt and rock the blade of the spatula in the icing, being careful to even it out and eliminate any air bubbles.

**3** Smooth round the cake in a fan pattern, turning the cake and drawing the spatula out from the center to the edges. Flatten the fan pattern in two or three sweeps, using the turntable and keeping the spatula still.

**4** Take a straight-edge or a ruler, longer than the diameter of the cake. Hold it at either end, tilt it at an angle to the cake and pull it smoothly across the surface to the edge of the cake. Pivot the straight-edge so that its other long edge is in contact with the icing and push it gently away from you. You should have icing sticking only to one face of your straight-edge. Maintain an even and steady pressure with both hands as you move the straight-edge over the cake.

If, after one sweep, you do not have a smooth surface, repeat the process.

If you still do not have a smooth top after three or four attempts, remove as much icing as is practical. Beat the mixture and start again from Step 2. Do not despair since the first coat need not be immaculate. It does not even matter if it is so thin that you can see the marzipan through it, all you need to do is to create a smooth seal. The second coat will hide any minor flaws and give you a perfect base for the following coat.

**5** When working on the sides of a cake use a stainless steel smoother or plain icing comb to remove the excess icing. A plastic one might bend with the weight of the icing. Hold the spatula at an angle against the side of the cake and rotate the turntable. As the icing piles up on the smoother or comb, scrape it into the bowl of unused icing.

**6** To cover the sides, take some icing on the metal spatula and rock it backwards and forwards on the cake as you rotate the turntable. Keep the spatula in the icing so that it is pushed forwards on to the marzipan to eliminate any air bubbles. Repeat the process until the sides are completely coated and have a reasonably smooth finish.

**1** Place the cake on a turntable. With a metal spatula, put the equivalent of two or three tablespoons of icing in the center of the cake. The blade of the spatula should be about 8 inches long.

**7** Smooth the sides of the cake in one continual sweep. Start with both hands on the furthest side of the cake, holding the spatula in one and the turntable in the other.

**8** Rotate the turntable towards you so that your hands meet up at their starting point. When the circle is completed, pull the smoother or icing comb off gently towards you.

**9** Go around once more with the smoother or icing comb to neaten the joint between the sides and top of the cake.

**10** Allow the icing to dry. Using a very sharp knife, gently carve away the rough edge of icing at the joint. Apply the second and third coats in the same way, letting each coat dry for about 6 hours.

**11** To cover the cake board, put some icing on the board with your metal spatula and rotate the turntable, dragging the icing around it for about 4 inches. Repeat the process all around the board.

**12** Use the smoother or icing comb to finish off and stop the icing building up around the sides of the cake. Hold the smoother or comb still and rotate the turntable with your other hand, smoothing all around the board in one sweep.

**13** Hold the metal spatula at an angle to the board and rotate the turntable to trim off any icing the spatula has pushed over the edge.

*Rough icing is particularly suitable for Christmas cakes where the textured surface is used to resemble snow.*

## ROUGH ICING

If you are icing a cake for the first time and are unable to get the icing smooth, you can always turn it into rough icing. This method is also useful if you want to ice a cake in a hurry.

**1** Put the royal icing on the cake as before and use a paddling motion with the metal spatula to bring it out to the edges of the cake. Pull up peaks of icing all over the cake with the flat side of a knife.

**2** Alternatively, use a slightly damp but not wet piece of foam rubber. This will give a lighter, more delicate texture than the knife.

# COVERING WITH FONDANT ICING

Cold rolled fondant or sugar paste has a big advantage over royal icing – it can be used to cover a cake in a single operation. In an emergency, it may even be applied without marzipan, though the results may not be as smooth. Marzipan the cake and leave it for two or three days for the surface to harden, then make the fondant (see p. 40). When rolling out a fondant, make sure that you do not have too much confectioner's sugar on the counter or it will cause the paste to dry out. Use only enough confectioner's sugar to prevent the fondant from sticking to the counter.

**1** To color the fondant, dip a wooden pick into the food coloring and draw it across the surface of the fondant a number of times. Do not dig holes in the fondant or you may introduce pockets of air which do not become apparent until the fondant has beeen rolled out for application to the cake.

**2** Knead the fondant in a circular motion to distribute the color evenly. For a marbled effect, stop kneading before the color has spread evenly through the paste.

**3** To test that you have an even color, cut the fondant ball in half. If it is full of deeply colored swirls and lines, you will need to knead it again, as the color is not evenly distributed. Knead and test again – this time the result should be perfect.

**4** Use alcohol or water to adhere the fondant to the marzipan. Many people use brandy or rum for flavor, or sherry for economy. The alcohol helps to sterilize the surface of the cake and improves the flavor. The cake should be placed on a sheet of wax paper to stop the counter getting sticky. Moisten the cake all over – if you leave any spaces uncovered, air bubbles may form there. Remove the paper and put the cake on the counter on a dusting of confectioner's sugar.

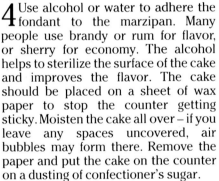

**5** Roll out the fondant icing on a dusting of confectioner's sugar. To pick up the paste, put your left palm underneath it and lay your right palm on the other side.

**6** Drape the fondant over your right hand and arm. Put your left hand and arm inside the fold of the fondant so that you can support it flat on both hands and arms.

**7** Lay the fondant over the cake so that the side furthest away from you touches the counter. Smooth it carefully over the top of the cake exactly as you did the marzipan (see p. 89).

**8** To obtain a really smooth glossy finish to the fondant icing use a large plastic smoother or plain icing comb. Hold it in your left hand, press down firmly with your right hand and move it from side to side across the top of the cake.

*Crimpers are used to make border patterns in fondant icing RIGHT. They are simple to handle and create a very consistent, attractive effect.*

**9** For the sides of the cake, hold the cake steady with the large smoother or plain icing comb to avoid finger-marks. Using a smaller-handled smoother icing comb with a beveled edge, smooth over the sides and round the corners of the cake.

**10** The smoothing process may create a few air pockets on top of the icing. If it does, prick them with a pin, going diagonally through the fondant to the marzipan. Smooth the top once the air has been pushed out.

**11** Gently push the cake to the edge of the counter using a smoother or plain icing comb and then support the base of the cake on the palm of your hand. Hold it over the cakeboard and quickly withdraw your hand, allowing the cake to drop on to the board below. Adjust the cake to its final position using the smoothers or icing combs. Note that the cake is secured to the board with a piece of fondant placed in the center just before the cake is put on to it. When it is in place, press down on the top of the cake with the large smoother or icing comb to flatten the ball of fondant and secure the cake to the board.

**12** While the fondant is still soft, crimp the cake. Crimpers, mar-zipan nippers or clippers are useful tools for impressing a pattern into fondant icing. They are available with nine different patterns. Draw out the design you want to use and pin the paper pattern to the cake, then copy the design on to the cake. Remove the pattern and put a ribbon round the cake as a guide for maintaining a horizontal line. Remember not to release the crimpers too quickly or pull them away too fast or you will tear the fondant. They are very easy to use and with half an hour's practice on a piece of fondant you will be skilled enough to produce quite a professionally decorated cake, similar to the Golden Wedding Cake on p. 168.

# PASTRY BAGS

For intricate decorating work, paper pastry bags are essential. They are far superior to the syringe variety, as they are so much more flexible to handle.

If you are doing multi-colored work or using different tips, have several pastry bags ready.

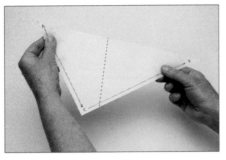

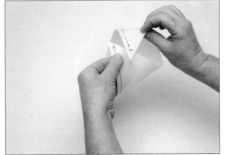

## MAKING A PASTRY BAG

Making paper pastry bags for fine decorative work is not difficult. Use wax paper or use packs of ready-cut paper available from specialist sources (see List of Suppliers, p. 224).

**1** Cut a 10-inch square of wax paper. Fold it in half diagonally to make a triangle. Mark points (A), (B) and (C) in the corners as illustrated in the diagrams below.

**2** With the point of the triangle (C) facing towards you and holding the triangle at points (A) and (B), fold (B) round and back over (A).

**3** Hold point (A) firmly and pull point (B) towards you to complete the cone shape. Take point (B) round to meet point (C).

**4** To secure the pastry bag, fold in the loose ends over the top edge and staple them together.

## FILLING A PASTRY BAG

**1** Cut off the end of the pastry bag and insert the required tip (see p. 86).

**2** Hold the pastry bag in your left hand with your thumb at the back for support.

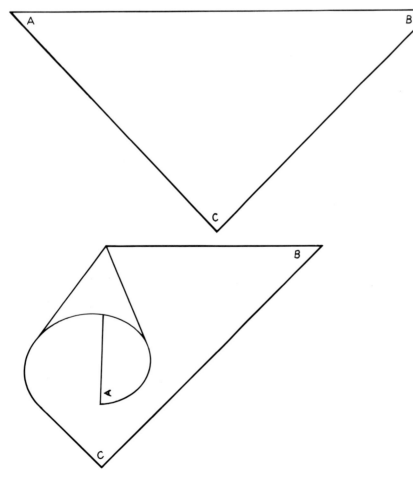

**3** Using a metal spatula, fill the bag half to two-thirds full. Push the icing down into the back of the bag against your thumb. Take care not to overfill as the icing may overflow from the top or the bag may burst.

**4** With your thumb, push the back of the bag right down over the icing.

**5** Carefully fold the sides of the bag in towards the center then fold over the top, pushing the icing down gently towards the tip. Fold over one corner again, making a pad to push with your thumb.

---

### HANDY HINT

Have a damp cloth at hand to wipe the tip in between pipings and to help stop it from getting clogged with hardened icing. If using several bags to decorate a cake, always cover the ends of them when not in use with a damp cloth or stand them tip downwards in a pastry bag stand containing a dampened piece of foam rubber.

---

## HOLDING A PASTRY BAG

**1** Hold the pastry bag between your middle and index fingers and push with your thumb.

**2** Place the end of the tip in position over the work, before beginning to push the icing through the bag. Pressing down with your thumb on the folded part of the bag, squeeze out the icing. Pressing with and releasing your thumb will cause the icing to flow, then stop. Because the icing continues to flow after the pressure has stopped, you must release the pressure on the bag before you reach the end of the line to be piped. If you watch carefully to see how the icing flows, you will quickly learn to judge the pressure and movement required to produce even, well-formed lines and shapes.

**3** Once you have mastered piping straight lines, try using a star tip for shells. Insert tip No. 5 into the pastry bag. Position the tip on the surface where you want to pipe the shell. Without moving the bag, push out the icing. Once the shell has formed, pull the bag back to form a tail. Position the bag to form the next shell so that it just overlaps the tail of the first one.

---

*Practise with a large plain tip, No. 2 or 3, to begin with and then star tip No. 5, BELOW, until you feel confident handling a pastry bag.*

# PIPING TECHNIQUES

The consistency of the icing is the most important factor in piping. It should not be too stiff – it must be light and fluffy and it must hold a peak.

## STARS

Stars can be piped with tips Nos. 5, 7, 9, 11, 12, 13 or 15. Hold the bag, fitted with the appropriate tip, perpendicular to the surface to be iced. Press on the bag to release the icing, then pull it up gently to form a paint and a star shape will be formed.

## ROSETTES

You can use Nos. 42, 43 and 44. These rosettes are made with fine rope tips, which have shallower indentations than the star tips. With the bag held perpendicular to the surface to be iced, pipe a circle. Lift the tip slightly, apply pressure, bring it round to the center and release the pressure as you tail it off.

## SCROLLS

Pipe scrolls with fine rope tips, as for rosettes, but instead of tailing off into the circle, come out of it, creating a C- or an S-shape. For a C-shape, work in a counterclockwise motion. For an S-shape, take the tip round clockwise. You can make attractive patterns by combining the C and the S and, if you twist the tip as you pipe, you will get a rope effect.

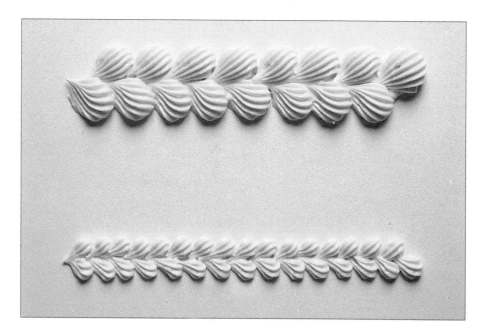

## ALTERNATING SHELLS

You can use tips Nos. 5 and 13. Follow the instructions for shells, but take the point down at an angle of 45 degrees. Pipe a second row of shells beneath the first, taking the points up. Start with your piping tip at the tail of the upper shell for a braided effect.

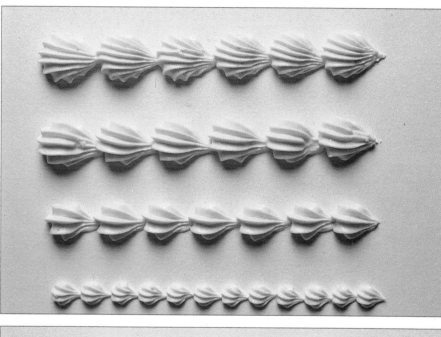

## SHELLS

You can use tips Nos. 13, 11, 8 and 5. Rest the appropriate tip on the surface where you want to pipe the shell. Push out the icing without moving the bag. Once the shell has formed, pull the bag back to form a tail. Position the bag to form the next shell so that it just overlaps the tail of the one in front.

## FLEUR - DE - LIS

This shape can be piped with a shell tip No. 13 (above) or fine rope tip Nos. 44, 43 or 42 (below) or you can even use a plain round tip for a smooth effect. First pipe a shell with a long tail. Then pipe an S-shape scroll to the left and a C-shape scroll to the right. You can pipe the flowers in the same way. Pipe one set of petals and overpipe the second set.

## STRAIGHT LINES

You can use tips Nos. 4, 3, 2, 1 and 0. Touch the surface where you want to pipe. Lift the tip and apply pressure so that the icing flows out in a straight line. Drop it down at the other end of the line after you have released the pressure and the icing has stopped flowing. Do not attempt to pipe a straight line by dragging the tip along the surface of the cake or wax paper. All you will succeed in doing is damaging the fine edge of the tip and indenting the surface of the cake. The tip must be lifted off the surface.

Overpiping is a classic piping technique. It takes practice and requires a very steady hand. By piping straight lines of varying widths touching each other, you can create a classic three-dimensional effect. Let each line dry before you begin on the next. If you are using this technique on a wedding cake, complete all your piping with one width tip before you change to the next. If you make a mistake, you can correct it with a slightly damp paintbrush, by pushing the line back into shape.

## TRELLIS

You will need tip No. 1. Pipe one set of parallel lines, then overpipe a second either at right angles for squares, or with both sets of lines on the diagonal for diamonds. Use another width tip for overpiping to create a different effect.

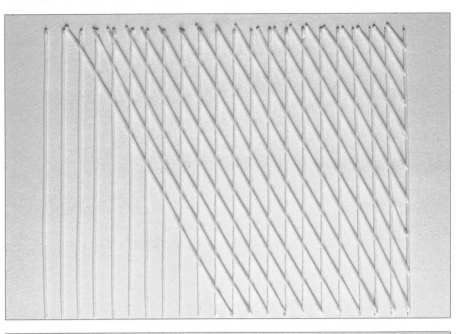

## ZIGZAGS

You can use tips Nos. 42, 5 or 3. These can be piped in a continuous line with any shaped tip. Until you are more confident, you may find it easier to stop and start at each point – this will give a very definite V-shape to the zigzag.

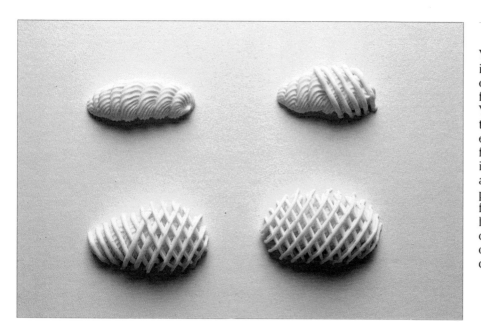

## RAISED TRELLIS OR NETS

You can use tips Nos. 43, 3, 2 and 1. This is a style that was very popular a couple of decades ago. It has now gone out of fashion because it is time-consuming. You can build up from the base with trellis work, but it is quicker and just as effective to pipe an oval scroll with a fine rope tip and cover it. Anchor the icing, twist the tip to form a rope as you apply the pressure, then release the pressure and taper off. Overpipe with a fine round tip, making parallel diagonal lines. Overpipe again in the opposite direction. You can build up the net by overpiping with decreasing sized tips in different directions.

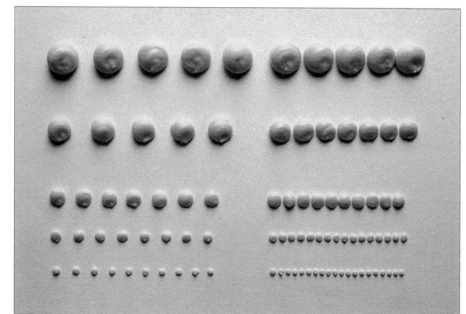

## DOTS AND BEADS

You can use tips Nos. 4, 3, 2, 1 and 0. The difficulty with piping dots and beads is disguising the take-off point, which will tend to make a tail. This is harder to disguise, the bigger the bead you are piping. Using constant pressure keep the point of the tip stationary in the bead until it is the size required. Release pressure on the bag after piping the bead and then take off gently to the side. Correct any mistakes with a slightly dampened brush once the bead is nearly dry by gently pressing any projecting point down into the mass of icing. The larger beads are almost always overpiped, as on the Easter Cake (see p. 132) and the Traditional Birthday Cake (see p. 152).

## TWISTED ROPE

You can use tips Nos. 44, 43, 42 and 5. Twisted rope can be piped with a plain writing tip or a shell tip as well as a rope tip. The trick is to twist the bag as you are piping. Keep constant pressure on the bag. To avoid varying the width of the rope, hold the bag at an angle and rotate it as you go.

## BASKET WEAVING

Basket weaving looks very attractive round the sides of a cake (see the Mother's Day Cake on p. 128). You will need a special basket weaving tip (No. 22) as well as a plain round tip. Pipe a vertical line with the plain tip. Pipe short lines across it with the basket weaving tip leaving the width of the tip between each line. Pipe a second vertical line down the side of the 'basket work' parallel to the first and just covering the ends of the basket work. Go back to the basket tip and fill in the gaps between the first and the second vertical line, taking the weave over the second line to where the third vertical line will be piped, parallel to the second. Repeat all round the cake.

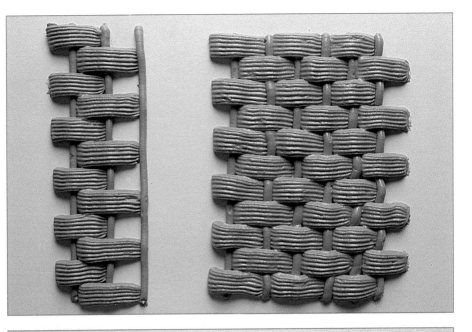

## CORNELLI

You will need nozzle tip No. 1. Cornelli or scribbling is an attractive texturing technique achieved by piping a maze of W-shapes and M-shapes in a continuous line but at random over a confined space. Use a fine tip and avoid moving in straight lines – you should not be able to see where the work begins or ends.

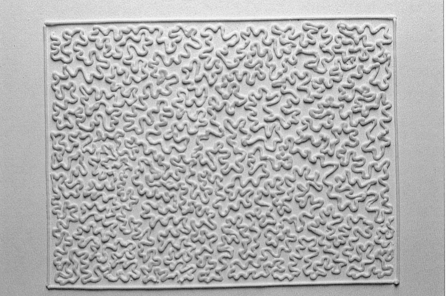

## EMBROIDERY

Embroidery work makes a very attractive decoration for the side of a cake. The illustration shows a complete pattern and then the elements that make it up. Use tip No. 0 or 1 and pipe a row of blue built-up circles 1 inch apart. Pipe two similar circles above the first, two below the second and so on, alternating throughout the pattern. This is a reliable method of achieving an even pattern. Pipe a forget-me-not between each group of built-up circles. Finally add the leaves with green royal icing.

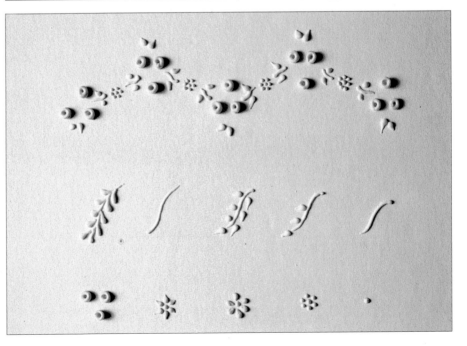

100

# MAKING LACE

Lace is always the last decoration to be added to a cake because it is so fragile and breaks so easily. Take great care when handling lace or when moving a cake with lace attached.

Designs for lacework are simple and varied. Several designs are included in the Templates Section (pp. 194-219) which can be traced off. Alternatively you can design your own lace. Patterns with several joints are stronger than those where the lines cross in only one or two places.

Lace is piped separately on to wax paper, left to dry, then carefully lifted off and attached to the cake with fine lines of royal icing.

**1** Choose a pattern and copy it 40 to 80 times on to a 6 inch square piece of tracing paper, depending on the size of the lace. Use a sharp pencil or fine fiber tip pen. Each piece of lace is ½ inch wide, so it is easy to work out how much you will need. Six sheets with 40 to 80 pieces of lace will be enough for a three-tiered wedding cake. It is a good idea, however, to pipe half as many pieces again as you will actually need if you are a beginner, because you are likely to break several pieces.

**2** Tape the four corners of the tracing paper securely to a counter. Tape a larger piece of wax paper over the pattern with masking tape. Only use a couple of pieces so that you do not disturb the piped lace too much when you remove the tape.

**3** With tip No. 0 or 1, pipe the lace in any direction that feels comfortable. Ensure that each piece of lace has a flat bar where it is to be attached to the cake. Wipe the end of the tip with your fingers or a damp cloth between each piece of lace to ensure clean lines. For particularly elaborate lace, use different colored icing for different sections of each piece. The bar should be the same color as the icing on the cake.

**4** If you make a mistake, it can be corrected with a fine paintbrush. The paintbrush should be slightly dampened, but not wet.

**5** Let the lace dry for at least two hours or overnight if possible. Do not put the lace in the oven to dry as the wax paper will melt into the icing.

**6** To remove the lace, curl the wax paper over the index finger of your left hand. The lace will begin to release. Slide a metal spatula under the piece of lace and gently lift it off. Never try to remove lace with tweezers, as the slightest pressure will break the lace. The lace is now ready to attach to the cake.

# RUN-OUTS

This technique involves piping an outline and flooding it, giving a good flat shape with cleanly rounded edges. It is also called flooding or running. The run-outs are usually piped on wax paper, left to dry then lifted off and used to decorate the cake. However, in some cases it is simpler to pipe run-out designs directly on to the cake, especially if the design is a figure or fairly complicated shape.

## ICING FOR RUN-OUTS

When you make up royal icing for run-outs, it should be to normal piping consistency. It should not be too moist or the icing will not set quickly and will be too weak. Make it in the normal way, then thin it down a little with beaten egg white or water. If you use egg white, the icing will be stronger, but it may take up to a week to dry. It is better to use water and add it, literally, a drop at a time. Use an eye dropper to get the consistency exactly right. Do not beat the icing as you are adding the water because you will incorporate too much air. Just stir it gently.

Add enough water so that your icing

is of a piping consistency. To judge the amount of water to add, swirl a knife in the bowl and count steadily to 10 as the ripples subside. The icing should just have found its own level as you get to 10 (about 5 seconds).

Icing collars, filigree pieces and designs that are subsequently lifted before placing in position are always piped on to wax paper, over an outline. The outline obviously acts as a guide, but its other purpose is to stop the flooded icing from contracting as it dries – not to stop it spreading. It will only spread if your icing is too runny.

It is important to dry run-outs as quickly as possible in order to get a good sheen or surface finish. A warm cupboard is often a good place.

## PIPING A RUN-OUT

**1** The first step in making a run-out is to secure a piece of wax paper to a counter over the outline you want to fill in. Attach a tag to the paper on which the outline is drawn, so you can easily slide it out from the wax paper afterwards. Do not use parchment paper as a substitute for wax, as it may

wrinkle. Draw the outline with a dark colored fiber tip or a sharp pencil. Put the paper wax side up to facilitate the release of the run-out when it dries. Use masking tape, which pulls off more easily than conventional scotch tape, to secure it. Wrenching away a piece of adhesive tape may break your run-out. Do not tape right around the wax paper – you may trap air underneath and the damp icing on top will cause the paper to lift and buckle the run-out as it dries. Secure the paper only at the corners.

**2** If you are piping a collar, or anything with a middle hollow (see the Celebration Cake, p. 170), make a small cut in the shape of a cross in the center of the paper to relax the natural tension in the fabric of the paper.

**3** Pipe the outline carefully following the line of the pattern on the tracing beneath.

**4** Fill a pastry bag with flooding icing, but do not cut the hole in the bottom until you are ready to make the run-out, or the icing will pour straight out ot it. Make sure that the hole you cut is not too big or you might lose control. A tip is not necessary for flooding.

**5** Start close to your outline, but do not touch it with the bag, or you may break it. Keeping the tip of the bag in the icing to reduce the chance of air bubbles forming, allow the icing to flow out, moving the bag backwards and forwards across the shape as you do so.

**6** When you have almost filled the whole area, use a paintbrush to push the icing right out to the edge of the line, so that it just spills on to it. This way you get a good smooth edge.

**7** Make sure there are no air bubbles in the icing by gently tapping the board on the counter. When any appear, smooth them away with your brush.

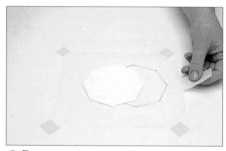

**8** Remove the pattern from beneath the paper by the tag. If you are making a whole series of run-outs, you can use the same pattern each time. Let the run-outs dry.

**9** Once a run-out is dry, you can remove it from the paper by working a cranked metal spatula (one with a thin angled blade) underneath it all the way round or by peeling the paper off the back, taking care not to break the run-out. With a large collar, the easiest way to peel off the backing is to pull it down, away from the run-out over the edge of the counter. Work half way round until the run-out is nearly free. Then turn it through 180 degrees and peel off the other side.

## MONOGRAMS AND NUMBERS

The important thing to decide here is which part of the design should be the most prominent. Pipe the back of the design first.

In the monogram 'NC', the visible parts of the C are piped first, because the N lies on top of it.

In the number 8, the crossover bar is slightly raised, so this should be piped last. Do not try and do it all at once, or it will merge into a completely flat shape.

## BUTTERFLIES

First pipe the inside of the wings with cornelli or other fine piping work. Then pipe the outline of the wings and flood first the bottom part and then the top.

When the wings are dry, pipe a teardrop-shaped piece of icing for the body. Attach the wings to it while it is still wet and support them with cotton balls until they have set in position. Use stamens for antennae, but remember that they are not edible.

### BELLS

Pipe the insides of the bells first and let them dry. Then pipe the top of the underneath bell. When that has dried, pipe the uppermost bell. The result is three-dimensional.

### ROSE

Start from the back of the design and work forwards, building it up in layers. As each step dries, fill in the next. Then finally fill in the center petals.

### FLOWER

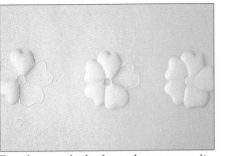

For the maple leaf, work on opposite sides of the flower, which will not touch each other, before flooding the inside petals. When all five petals are dry, pipe in the center.

### LEAVES

For holly and rose leaves, pipe the outline, flood half the leaf and let it dry, then flood the other half. The maple leaf is piped in four parts, letting each dry separately, to give a veined effect.

### SHIELD AND OVAL

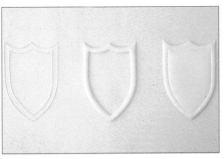

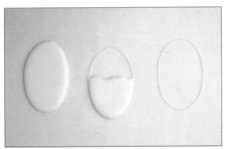

These are simple designs, popular on cakes for club occasions. Pipe the outline, then flood in the center. To give the shield a frame the flooding goes upwards, but not over the outline.

*If a run-out lies flat on a royal-iced cake, it can be piped directly on to the cake, as with the giraffe motif BELOW on the Boy's Christening Cake (see p. 144). The royal icing will hold the run-out in position.*

## SWANS

These swans are double-flooded, that is, flooded on the front and back, so they can be viewed from both sides. Their wings are piped and then the birds are assembled on a flooded base.

**1** First pipe the outline on wax paper. Work on the rear bird first. Once the icing has lost its wet look and is dry enough to hold the line, flood the body of the rear swan and the head of the front swan.

**2** Once the flooded icing has set, flood the body of the front swan. When the front swan has set, flood the head of the back swan, so that it lies over the head of the front swan and their necks are entwined.

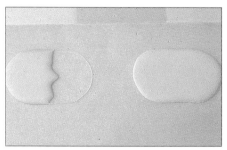

**3** Pipe an outline for the base and flood it. Remember to keep the end of the tip in the icing. Take the icing right up to the piping line and brush it on to, but not right over, the line.

**4** Pipe the wings with a No. 3 tip, which is one of the larger round tips. Start at the base of the wing and pipe right up to the wing tip. Continue the line down to the base and back out to the wing tip again. Go back down beside this second line, and up to the tip again. This time continue the piping down to the center of the wing and back out to the edge, to give the effect of feathers. Continue doing this until you get to the base of the wing. Each feather should be just touching the one beside it. Increase the pressure on the pastry bag at the tips of the feathers. When you reach the base, make a swirl to give strength to the wing at the point where it will be attached to the body. Pipe all four wings in the same way.

**5** Once the swans are completely dry, lift them off the wax paper with a cranked metal spatula and turn them over. Pipe a little icing into the centers of the bodies and up the neck to stop them sagging when they dry. Flood the back of the swans in the same order that you flooded the front (see Steps 1 and 2). Let the swans dry completely before painting the beak and eyes with orange and black food color on both sides.

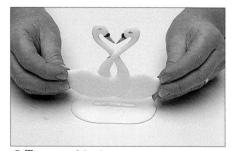

**6** To assemble the swans, pipe a line of royal icing, using tip No. 3 or No. 5, along the length of the base and set the swans down on to it.

**7** Pipe a dab of icing on each side of each swan and attach the wings. Support them until they are dry with cotton balls.

**8** Choose ribbons and flowers for dressing the swans in colors to match your cake. Make the ribbon loops (see p. 77) and assemble the flower sprays (see p. 76) and pieces of tulle caught into bunches with twisted wire.

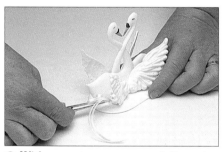

**9** With your tweezers, carefully put a small piece of slightly dampened fondant icing behind the swan's wing. Be careful not to over-dampen the fondant icing or it will melt the royal icing.

**10** With the tweezers, carefully press the ribbon loops, flower sprays and tulle into the fondant ball. As the fondant dries, it will secure them.

# PIPED FLOWERS

You can use tips Nos. 57, 58 or 59. Piping flowers is no more difficult than the other techniques described here, though the results look very sophisticated. To give the petals strength you will need to work with slightly thicker icing than that used for piping shells. Flowers can be piped on to either a cone or squares of wax paper stuck with icing on an icing nail.

You will need a petal tip, which is basically flat with a slightly scooped opening where the icing is squeezed, but with one end slightly wider than the other to give flare to the petals.

## ROSE

1 Take a cone of marzipan, making sure it has dried thoroughly before you start to work. Pipe a tight little center to the rose with tip No. 57, 58 or 59 by putting the thick end of the tip down on to the marzipan and piping all round the end of the cone. Rotate the cone in your left hand to do this. Let the icing dry between steps.

2 For the next layer, pipe three tiny petals, each one going a third of the way around the cone and slightly overlapping the one before. Angle the tip outwards as you go, to get the petals to curve.

3 Starting at the center of one of these petals, make a second row. Keep the thick side of the tip down and the thin side up. Pipe four or five petals for the outer layer.

If you are making about a dozen roses at a time, the petals on the first rose will be dry by the time you come to the last one – this way you need not stop working.

For a two-tone rose, pipe the outer petals a shade lighter, or darker, than the inner ones. For a variegated rose, streak the icing in the bag with two or more different shades.

Once the roses are dry cut off the marzipan cones with a sharp knife.

## APPLE BLOSSOM

For this technique you will need a nail, which is a disc of metal on a spike, tip No. 57, 58 or 59 and a small square of wax paper for every flower you pipe. If you do not have an icing nail, you could use the top of a cork stuck on to a skewer.

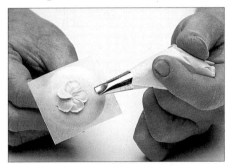

1 Put a dab of icing on the head of the nail and press it into the center of the wax paper. Let it dry so that the paper does not slip while you are working.

2 Use the petal tip with the thick edge towards the center of the flower. Increase the pressure on the bag as you turn the nail and slightly lift the thin edge of the tip as you form each petal.

3 After you have made the first petal, wipe the end of the tip clean. Then tuck the tip underneath the edge of the first petal and make another one just as you did before, releasing the pressure before you take it off.

4 Continue until you have five petals. You can decorate the center of the flower with a little bead of yellow icing, but be careful about putting small pieces of wire for stamens in a tiny flower like this – they are not edible.

*Rose*

## HYACINTH

You will need tip No. 37. First pipe the stem and the leaves in green icing. Then pipe two rows of tiny flowers, about five in a row, on either side of the stem. When these have dried, pipe a third row directly over the stem, giving a three dimensional effect. Add a final green leaf at the front of the flower.

*Hyacinth*

## PRIMROSE

You will need tip No. 57, 58 or 59. Pipe primroses as for apple blossom, but indent each of the petals slightly as you go. Pipe halfway up the petal, bring the tip back down towards you, then continue the curve, making a heart-shaped petal. Pipe five petals, tucking each one just underneath the one before. Pipe the center with a yellow dot and paint on green stamens. They make pretty Easter decorations for cakes and eggs.

*Primrose*

## PUSSY WILLOW

You will need tip No. 3 or 4. First pipe the branches in dark green or brown. Then, with white icing, pipe teardrop shapes, tailing back to join the ends of the branches. Finally, pipe a little V-shape at the base of each teardrop in brown.

*Pussy willow*

## VIOLET

You will need tip No. 57, 58 or 59. For a violet, pipe three larger purple petals at the top and two smaller ones underneath. A dot of yellow icing forms the center of the flower.

*Violet*

## NARCISSUS

Pipe these as for apple blossom, but make six white petals of a slightly more elongated shape, piping up and down the petal rather than straight around it. With the side of a dampened brush, mark the lines going to and from the center of the flower. Dot the center with orange icing. For a daffodil, build up the center of the flower into a trumpet by holding the mouth of the tip vertically. Rotate the icing nail in your left hand so that you are piping a cylinder about ¼ inch high. Pull off gently with the tip in a horizontal position.

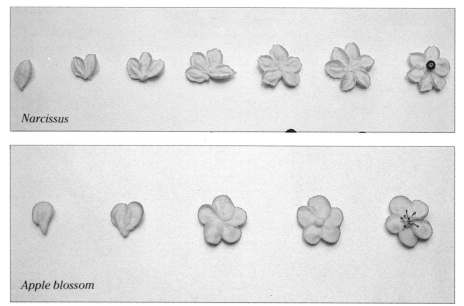

*Narcissus*

*Apple blossom*

## PANSY

Using the icing nail, make the first petal as for the apple blossom (see p. 106). Then pipe a second petal to overlap the first. Exerting pressure and shaking the piping tip slightly will help to give each petal a frilly edge.

The third and fourth petals are piped to the left and right sides respectively of the first pair of petals and each must overlap the edges of the first pair.

After piping the fourth petal, turn the nail through 180 degrees and pipe the final petal, starting from the center of the flower. This is a large petal which must overlap the sides of the two small petals adjacent to it. It should have a frilly edge.

The key to making successful pansies is to pivot the petal tip around a central point, so that the thicker end of the tip is almost stationary while the outside edge rotates from the outer edge of the petal.

## SWEET PEA

Using wax paper on a piping nail, make

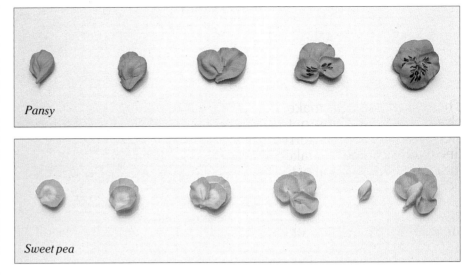

*Pansy*

*Sweet pea*

the first petal fairly large, using similar techniques as for the apple blossom or pansy. Then pipe the second petal to overlap the first almost completely. The third and fourth petals are piped to the right and left respectively of the first pair.

The center petal or pod is piped in one motion by holding the tip so that the axis of its opening is ranged straight up the center line of the flower. With the end of the tip held just a little above the petals, squeeze the bag gently and move the tip towards the top of the flower. Increase the pressure and then draw the end of the bag towards the starting point, decreasing the pressure during the return stroke.

## PIPED FLOWER SPRAYS

*Violet*

*Narcissus*

*Apple blossom*

*Sweet pea*

# PIPED BORDERS

These pretty designs make charming decorations for the side of a cake. You can scribe a line lightly around the cake indicating the position of the border.

The first two are variations using a forget-me-not tip (No. 37), which you use in the same way as a star tip, simply pushing out a small amount of icing. Fill in the centers with yellow, pipe leaves with a fine tip and add a beaded border. For the hanging rose, start with the stems and leaves. Then pipe the flowers, starting with the back petal. Pipe the next petal to overlap the first slightly, the third tucked underneath it and brought forward and the fourth the same on the other side. Pipe a green calyx to join the flowers to the stems. For the grape border, pipe the stems and upper leaves, making tendrils by rotating the end of the tip in your hand. Add the purple grapes, bead by bead, then finish by piping more leaves to overlap the joints.

*Pink forget-me-not*

*Blue forget-me-not*

*Hanging rose*

*Grape*

# TEMPLATES FOR POSITIONING PILLARS

The overall effect of an elaborately tiered cake can easily be spoiled by incorrectly positioned supporting pillars. The diagrams in this section show you how to work out where to position pillars on different-shaped cakes. The principles involved for most of the shapes are the same.

Templates can be made from paper or thin card. To obtain a good shape in each case, either draw round the cake pan and cut the shape out just inside the line to allow for the thickness of the pan or make a paper pattern following the instructions for each shape. You will need to make one template the size of the bottom tier for a two-tiered cake and two templates the size of the bottom and middle tiers for a three-tiered cake.

For some shapes you can use either three or four pillars. Either method holds the weight of the tier above and it is a matter of deciding which you think looks better.

*The diagram BELOW applies to all shapes of cake. The points indicate how far each pillar should be positioned from the centre of the cake for 4 sizes of cake, for example on an 8-inch cake, each pillar should be 2½ inches from the center of the cake. This position will ensure maximum stability for the supported tier.*

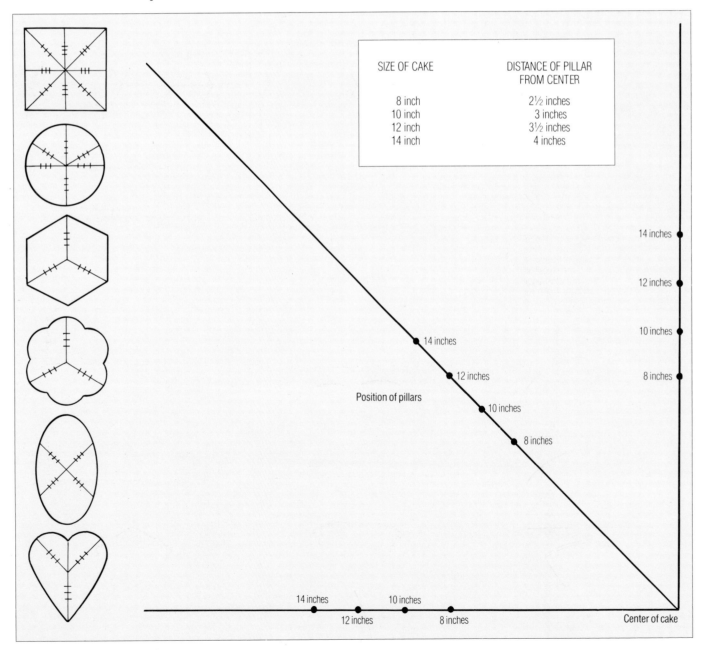

| SIZE OF CAKE | DISTANCE OF PILLAR FROM CENTER |
|---|---|
| 8 inch | 2½ inches |
| 10 inch | 3 inches |
| 12 inch | 3½ inches |
| 14 inch | 4 inches |

Position of pillars

Center of cake

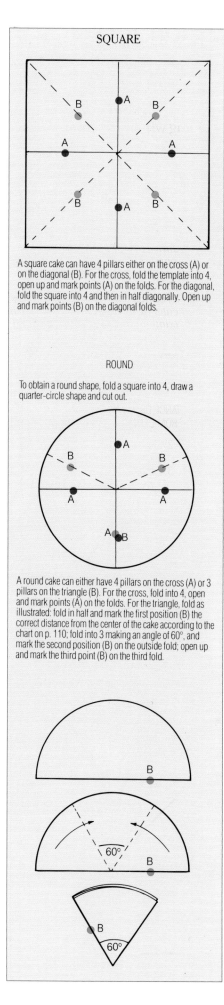

## SQUARE

A square cake can have 4 pillars either on the cross (A) or on the diagonal (B). For the cross, fold the template into 4, open up and mark points (A) on the folds. For the diagonal, fold the square into 4 and then in half diagonally. Open up and mark points (B) on the diagonal folds.

## ROUND

To obtain a round shape, fold a square into 4, draw a quarter-circle shape and cut out.

A round cake can either have 4 pillars on the cross (A) or 3 pillars on the triangle (B). For the cross, fold into 4, open and mark points (A) on the folds. For the triangle, fold as illustrated: fold in half and mark the first position (B) the correct distance from the center of the cake according to the chart on p. 110; fold into 3 making an angle of 60°, and mark the second position (B) on the outside fold; open up and mark the third point (B) on the third fold.

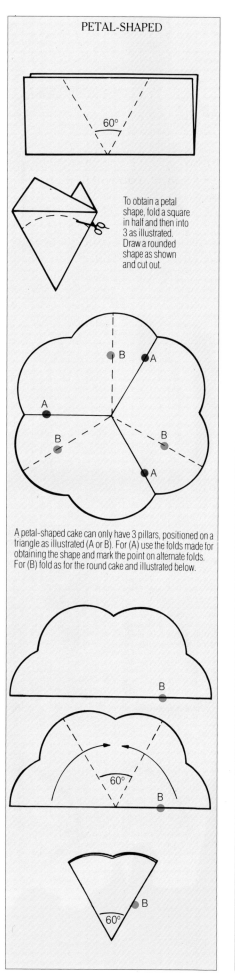

## PETAL-SHAPED

To obtain a petal shape, fold a square in half and then into 3 as illustrated. Draw a rounded shape as shown and cut out.

A petal-shaped cake can only have 3 pillars, positioned on a triangle as illustrated (A or B). For (A) use the folds made for obtaining the shape and mark the point on alternate folds. For (B) fold as for the round cake and illustrated below.

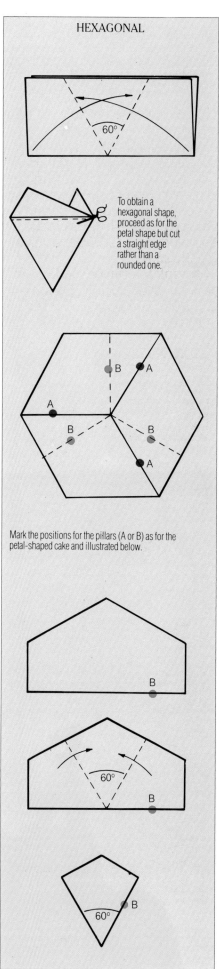

## HEXAGONAL

To obtain a hexagonal shape, proceed as for the petal shape but cut a straight edge rather than a rounded one.

Mark the positions for the pillars (A or B) as for the petal-shaped cake and illustrated below.

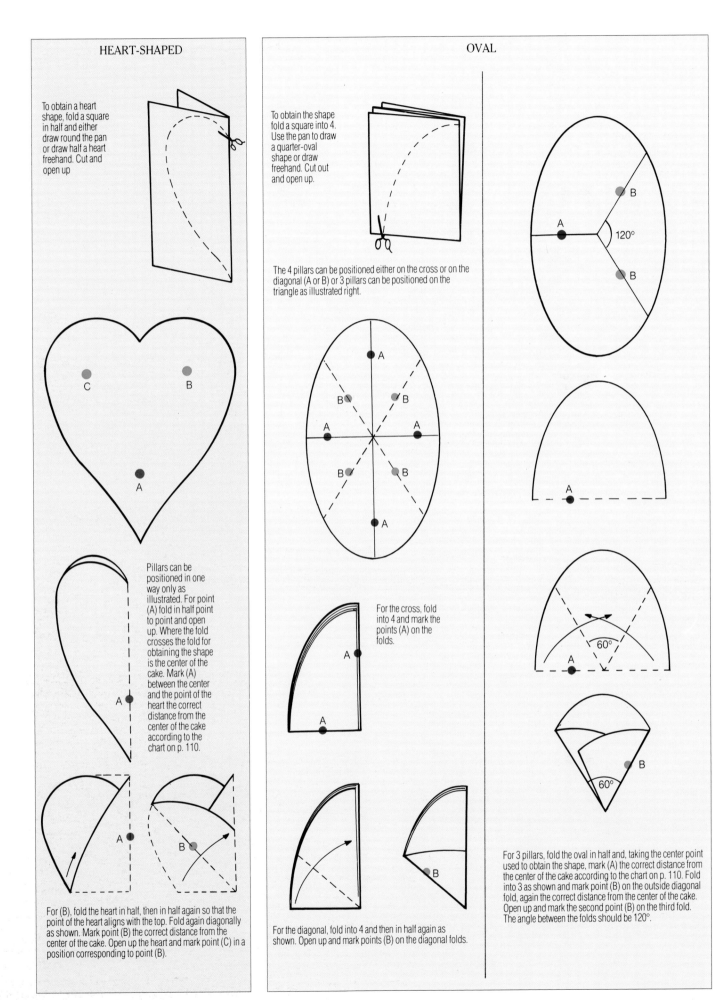

## HEART-SHAPED

To obtain a heart shape, fold a square in half and either draw round the pan or draw half a heart freehand. Cut and open up

Pillars can be positioned in one way only as illustrated. For point (A) fold in half point to point and open up. Where the fold crosses the fold for obtaining the shape is the center of the cake. Mark (A) between the center and the point of the heart the correct distance from the center of the cake according to the chart on p. 110.

For (B), fold the heart in half, then in half again so that the point of the heart aligns with the top. Fold again diagonally as shown. Mark point (B) the correct distance from the center of the cake. Open up the heart and mark point (C) in a position corresponding to point (B).

## OVAL

To obtain the shape fold a square into 4. Use the pan to draw a quarter-oval shape or draw freehand. Cut out and open up.

The 4 pillars can be positioned either on the cross or on the diagonal (A or B) or 3 pillars can be positioned on the triangle as illustrated right.

For the cross, fold into 4 and mark the points (A) on the folds.

For the diagonal, fold into 4 and then in half again as shown. Open up and mark points (B) on the diagonal folds.

120°

60°

60°

For 3 pillars, fold the oval in half and, taking the center point used to obtain the shape, mark (A) the correct distance from the center of the cake according to the chart on p. 110. Fold into 3 as shown and mark point (B) on the outside diagonal fold, again the correct distance from the center of the cake. Open up and mark the second point (B) on the third fold. The angle between the folds should be 120°.

# ASSEMBLING TIERS

It is very important for the stability of the finally assembled cake that the tiers are level. To ensure this, position the pillars on the cake and check whether the tops are horizontal with a spirit level. Make sure that you have a level counter before you begin. If the pillars are not horizontal, work from the highest pillar.

**1** Work out the position of the pillars on the template according to the instructions opposite. Put the template on the cake and use the scriber to mark where the pillars are to be positioned. Remove the template.

**2** To ensure that the cake will not collapse, the weight of the upper tiers is actually supported on wooden skewers.

**3** Place a wooden ruler or straight edge on top of the pillars and hold a skewer vertically alongside the cake with the tip of the skewer resting on top of the cake board. This way the measurements include the depth of the cake, the height of the pillars and the thickness of the ruler or straight edge.

**4** Mark the skewer with a pencil where it meets the top of the straight edge. This ensures that the approximate ⅛-inch thickness of the ruler or straight edge is the amount of the skewer which will protrude from the top of the pillar. The skewer for each cake should be marked and cut to the same length.

**5** To insert the skewers into the cakes, carefully push them into the icing, marzipan and cake until the point of the skewer reaches the cake board.

**6** Drop the pillar down over the skewer. It is important to ensure that the tops of the skewers are horizontal in relation to each other.

**7** Repeat the procedure for each cake. When you are storing the cakes, while you are working on them and when they are finished, do not put them in airtight containers or in a cold cupboard or refrigerator. Keep them at room temperature in cardboard boxes.

*It is well worth taking the time to position and assemble tiers correctly.*

# SECTION TWO

# FESTIVE CAKES

If you only make one cake a year, it will probably be a Christmas cake. No Christmas table is complete without a royal-iced rich fruit cake as its centerpiece. This section on Festive Cakes presents a choice of five Christmas cakes, included a simple, traditional design, an elegant star-shaped cake and an unusual Christmas cake disguised as a Christmas pudding.

This section covers several other festive occasions during the year which are traditionally celebrated with cakes: a heart-shaped cake for Valentine's Day, a basket of flowers for Mother's Day, a Simnel Easter cake and an iced Easter cake for Easter Sunday and finally an abundant cornucopia for Thanksgiving.

## AMERICAN CHRISTMAS CAKE

This very rich Christmas cake is made with candied fruit and baked in a ring-shaped pan.

### INGREDIENTS
candied 1×8-inch ring fruit cake (see p. 24)
1½ cups apricot glaze, redcurrant or blackcurrant jelly

### MATERIALS & DECORATIONS
1×10-inch round cake board
candied fruit and nuts
sprig of holly

**1** The recipe for this rich fruit cake includes candied fruit, dates, nuts, raisins and golden raisins. It should be baked for about 1½ hours or until it is firm to the touch, at 275°F. Let cool in

the pan for about 10 minutes, and then turn it out.

**2** Cut decorative shapes from candied fruit, such as pineapple rings, pears and cherries. When the cake has cooled, decorate it with the fruit and nuts. Brush it with apricot glaze, redcurrant or blackcurrant jelly and leave overnight. Give it another good coating of glaze the next day. The glaze helps to preserve the cake.

**3** Set the cake on the board. Give the cake and its decorations a final coat of glaze. Add a sprig of holly for a festive touch.

# SIMPLE CHRISTMAS CAKE

This simple but elegant Christmas cake adds a very professional touch to a display of Christmas food.

### INGREDIENTS
1 × 8-inch round rich fruit cake (see p. 23)
about 4⅓ cups Marzipan (see p. 27)
about 4 cups Royal Icing (see p. 38)
about 1 scant cup Marzipan or Fondant Icing (see pp. 27 and 40)

### MATERIALS & DECORATIONS
1 × 10-inch round cake board
pastry bag
tips Nos. 13, 57, 58 or 59
wooden picks
red ribbon
holly leaves (p. 69)
Food colors: red, yellow, brown

**1** Apply a coat of royal icing to the top and sides of the marzipanned cake. While the second application of icing of the cake is still wet, comb the sides of the cake to make a ridged pattern. Shells are piped at the top edge and the base of the cake with tip No. 13. When the icing has dried a bold red ribbon is attached to complete the side decorations.

**2** To make the candles for the top, roll a 12-inch sausage of red marzipan or fondant icing about ¼ inch in diameter. Remember to roll with the palms of your hands to get the sausage of icing smooth.

**3** Fold the sausage of icing in half. Twist it together to form a rope. You can also use this idea to decorate the base of the cake instead of a shell border if you prefer.

**4** Cut the rope into two pieces, one slightly longer than the other, to make the candles. Cut circles of yellow marzipan for the flames, using either a cutter or the end of a tip.

**5** Cut a crescent off the side of the circle to create a flame shape. When positioning the candles on the cake just dampen the icing slightly with a brush to hold them in place. Draw a halo of yellow or gold with food color or dusting powder, dampen the backs of the flames and stick them inside each halo. Paint the center of the flames red.

**6** Make a small cone of marzipan for each pine cone. Each finished cone will be double the size of the marzipan cone.

**7** Hold the cone by a wooden pick inserted into the flat end of the marzipan. Pipe across the top of the cone in one direction, then in the other to form a cross and build up the center point.

**8** With the thicker side of the tip pointing down, pipe the petals, lifting the tip slightly and rotating the cone as you go. Cover the whole cone, working in spirals down to the base.

**9** Let the cones dry before removing the wooden picks. For a variegated effect, streak the brown icing with yellow.

**10** Arrange the holly and position the pine cones around the base of the candles. Pipe a Christmas message if you wish.

# ELABORATE CHRISTMAS CAKE

Although this cake looks elaborate, it is quite simple to decorate. Ready-made decorations could be substituted for the Santa Claus face if time is short.

### INGREDIENTS
1 × 8-inch square rich fruit cake (see p. 23)
4⅓ cups Marzipan
about 3¼ cups Royal Icing (see p. 38)
about ¾ cup Royal Icing for flooding

### MATERIALS & DECORATIONS
1 × 10-inch square cake board
fine scriber
fine paintbrush
pastry bag
tips No. 1 or 2
silver balls
template (see pp. 194-219)
Food colors: red, pink, black, green, yellow, brown

**1** Marzipan and white flat ice the cake. Let dry. Transfer the Santa Claus face design on to the top of the cake. Scribe it on, or trace it through to the cake. For the beard take a tablespoon of stiff royal icing and place it on the cake in the center of the beard with a metal spatula.

**2** With a paintbrush spread the icing using a swirling motion to create the effect of a thick and curly beard. Do not fill in the moustache at this stage.

**3** Make the fur and pom-pom for the hat using stiff royal icing. Let dry overnight. When working in red and white, or any contrast colors, it is especially important to keep the cake in a dry atmosphere or the icing will absorb moisture and the darker colors may bleed into the lighter ones, spoiling the effect.

**4** Make some pink flooding icing to a count of 20 rather than 10 (see p. 102), in order to form the rest of the face. To pipe the face use a pastry bag and begin at the forehead, around the eyes and then the cheeks. As soon as the icing on the cheeks starts to form a crust, insert the point of the bag under the cheek and push some more icing into it to "blow" it up. When the cheeks are dry, pipe two beads to form the nostrils.

**5** Paint the mouth black and pipe a line of red icing to represent the bottom lip. Fill in the hat with red flooding icing of normal consistency (i.e. to a count of 10).

**6** When the nostrils are dry, pipe the bridge of the nose as a teardrop shaped bead at the bottom and taper it off towards the brow. Let dry. Add the moustache by piping a white 'S' shape at either side below the nose and swirling it with a paintbrush. Pipe the eyebrows. Paint the eyeballs with food color (not staring straight ahead) and laughter lines at the corners of the eyes. Pipe the holly and add the berries.

**7** For the sides of the cake you may work with edible ink fiber-tipped pens or the design may be painted on using a brush and food coloring. Outline the Christmas trees and houses all round the cake. Then, with a dampened brush, shade the outlines to add subtle color to the shapes.

**8** With flooding icing, again to a consistency of 20, put snow on the branches and roofs, using a metal spatula and stiff royal icing. With a normal consistency of royal icing, draw icicles off the edge of the cake. When these have dried, pipe fine icicles with tip No. 1 or No. 2. Then sprinkle the top of the cake with silver balls.

# CHRISTMAS PUDDING CAKE

The basis for this unusual Christmas cake is a spherical fruit cake. A spherical cake can also be decorated in other ways, for example as a football or tennis ball or as a fruit (see the Strawberry cake on p. 174).

### INGREDIENTS
1 × 2lb spherical rich fruit cake (see p. 23)
about 2 cups Marzipan (see p. 27)
about 2⅓ cups Fondant Icing (see p. 40)
generous ½ cup Royal Icing for flooding
  (see p. 38)

### MATERIALS & DECORATIONS
1 × 9-inch round cake board
turntable (optional)
modeling tool
fine paintbrush (or edible pens)
sprig real or artificial holly
Food colors: brown, red, green

**1** Use a 2lb spherical pan without paper lining to bake this cake. Make sure the pan is well greased and floured. If used for baking as a sphere, the pan should have a small hole in the top to allow the steam to escape when baked. Take the cake out of the pan while it is still hot – if you allow it to cool, the fats in the cake and around the pan will solidify and it will be difficult to remove without spoiling its shape.

**2** Drape the cake with marzipan, finishing it off neatly underneath. Let the marzipan dry for several hours. Then drape it with fondant icing, colored deep brown.

**3** To make the plate, cover a round 9-inch cake board with white fondant icing. Put it on the turntable and make the grooves with a knife or modeling tool.

**4** A U or V shaped tool makes an interesting molded edge. It is much easier to do this kind of decoration on a turntable.

**5** Paint a pattern on the edge of the plate to complete the effect, using the fine paintbrush and red and green food colors or red and green food color pens.

**6** When you have completed the molding, load the paintbrush with red food color or use a red food color pen. Position the brush or pen for the red ring on the plate, hold it there and spin the turntable slowly until the ring is completed.

**7** Place the cake on the plate and pour a small quantity of thick flooding icing made to a count of 20 over the top of the cake to create the effect of white sauce. Decorate the top with a sprig of real or artificial holly.

# STAR CAKE

This Star Cake makes an elegant and ususual Christmas cake. The basic design could be used for any occasion, with an appropriate central decoration.

## INGREDIENTS

1×8-inch star-shaped fruit cake (see p. 23 and Step 1)
about 2 lb Marzipan (see p. 27)
about 2 lb Fondant Icing (see p. 40)
about 8 oz Royal Icing (see p. 38)

## MATERIALS & DECORATIONS

1×10-inch hexagonal cake board
crimper No. 5
wax paper
pastry bag
tips Nos. 1 and 43
smoother or plain icing comb
template (see pp. 194-219)

---

### RELEASING PIPED SHAPES

If you have steady, cool, dry hands, you can simply hold the shape in your palm and peel back the wax paper. If your hands are hot or damp, the sugar may get sticky and the design may break. Instead you can put the paper and icing onto a flat surface (a turntable is used here), hold it down gently with a piece of cardboard and pull the paper down perpendicular to the flat surface. The icing will move forward as you peel the backing off. Do not go too far or it will drop from the card and shatter. Turn the paper round and work from the other end until the icing is completely free.

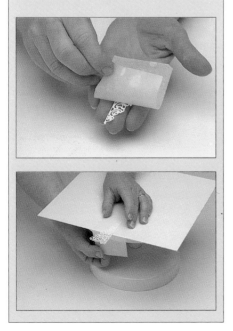

**1** Use a pan or frame in the shape of a star to make this cake. Alternatively you can make a round or square cake and carefully cut out the shape once the cake is completely cold. You can either drape marzipan over the cake or cut it out – a star shape for the top and a band for the side. The fondant icing covering is draped over the marzipan in one piece.

**2** Crimp a design round the sides of the cake about ½ inch from the top. Work from the concave points out towards the star's points, a section at a time. Crimp another border the same distance from the cake board.

**3** Attach a ribbon round the sides of the cake, securing it at the concave points with tiny dabs of royal icing. Pipe a shell border, using tip No. 43, round the base. With the edge of a smoother or plain icing comb, mark a star shape round the top of the cake.

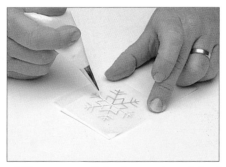

**4** Pipe a snowflake for each point of the star on to wax paper. When they are dry, turn them over and pipe the other side with tip No. 1.

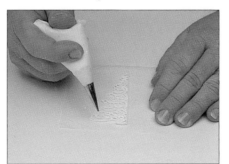

**5** Pipe the Christmas tree for the center of the cake in four sections. Turn the four sections over and pipe the reverse sides. When they are dry, assemble them by piping a line up the center post of one and sticking a second to it. Stick the cross pieces on

either side with two more lines of icing.

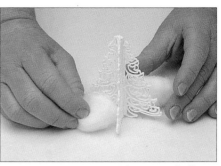

**6** Prop up the tree with cotton balls or rolled up pieces of kitchen towel and let dry overnight.

**7** Put the snowflakes in position, sticking them down with a little royal icing. Slip them into place with a metal spatula to avoid handling. Pipe a fine cross in the center of the cake and set the Christmas tree down on it. A fine line of icing is enough to hold the snowflakes and tree in position – if you use too much icing you will have to clean it up with a damp paintbrush in order to disguise the joint.

**8** If you want to store the cake for a while, keep the tree in a separate container. When you are ready to display the cake, put the tree in place and decorate the top of the tree with a piped star.

# VALENTINE CAKE

This elegant Valentine cake design could also be made to celebrate an engagement or anniversary.

### INGREDIENTS
8 inch heart-shaped cake (see p. 24 and Step 1)
about 4⅓ cups Marzipan (see p. 27)
about 3¼ cups Fondant Icing (see p. 40)
about ¾ cup Royal Icing (see p. 38)

### MATERIALS & DECORATIONS
12-inch heart-shaped cake board crimper No. 8
pastry bag
tips Nos. 4, 1, 57
red ribbon
pins
wax paper
12 piped red roses (see p. 106)
templates (see pp. 196-219)
Food colors: red and green

*Figure 1*          *Figure 2*

1 A heart-shaped cake can be achieved in one of three ways. It can be baked in a heart-shaped pan. It can be made from a square cake and a round cake (see Figure 1). It can be made from two rectangular cakes (see Figure 2). If you use the second or third method, sandwich the sides of the cake with marzipan for a fruit cake or buttercream for a sponge cake or madeira cake.

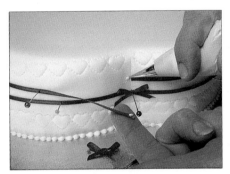

2 Cover the cake with marzipan and fondant icing. Crimp two borders of hearts around the edge. Pipe a tiny shell border at the base, using tip No. 4. To hold the ribbon in place, use pins with colored heads, so that you can spot them easily. Be careful not to lose any in the cake. It is better not to attempt to secure the ribbon all the way round with royal icing as it may discolor the ribbon and show through. Secure it in the cleft of the heart with icing and hold it with a pin. Pin all round, pulling the ribbon taut around the cake. Secure the joint with royal icing and conceal it with a tiny bow, held in place with royal icing. When dry remove all the pins.

3 Pipe a trellis heart on wax paper in two sections and let it dry. Remove it from the paper, then turn it over, and pipe the other side. Make the lace for the edges (see p. 101).

4 Pipe a dozen red roses (see p. 106) in advance. When ready to assemble the ornament fill a pastry bag with green icing to make the leaves. Cut a slit in the point of the bag.

5 Secure the inside rows of roses with royal icing, then pipe the leaves. To pipe a leaf, squeeze the icing out of the bag and move your hand backwards and forwards in minute steps as you draw the bag away from the starting point of the leaf, to make serrations around the edge. Stop the pressure and withdraw the bag – you will end with a pointed leaf. Repeat the process for the ouside rows.

6 Pipe a line of royal icing between the roses to anchor the heart. Place the two halves of the heart in position – the roses will prop them up as they dry.

7 For a very delicate finish attach the pieces of piped lace with royal icing to the edge of the heart.

# MOTHER'S DAY CAKE

This Basket of Flowers has been designed as a Mother's Day cake, but could also be made to celebrate a birthday or wedding anniversary.

### INGREDIENTS
1 × 8-inch round rich fruit cake (see p. 23)
warm apricot jam, mixed with a little water
about 12 oz Marzipan (see p. 27)
about 8 oz Royal Icing (see p. 38)
about 2½ lb Gelatin Icing (see p. 35)
about 4 oz Royal Icing for fixing (see p. 40)

### MATERIALS & DECORATIONS
1 × 9-inch round thin cake board
tip No. 47
pastry bag
stiff paper
artifical stamens
wooden pick
piece of curved wood or cardboard
gold ribbon
Food colors: brown, red, cream, yellow, green, edible gold luster

**1** Cut the cake with a small sharp knife into an oval shape. Spread the cake with warm apricot jelly. Roll out the marzipan and cover the cake. Let dry for 12 hours.

**2** Take ⅓ cup royal icing and color brown. Fit the tip into the pastry bag. Put approximatley ⅓ cup icing into the bag. Pipe the icing in ½-inch lengths pausing slightly between each movement to produce a basket-weave effect.

Refill the bag as necessary. Let dry for 12 hours.

**3** Take approximately 1¼ cups gelatin icing to make the tulips. This will make six tulips. Cut a petal shape from still paper. Roll out the icing round the petal template. Let each petal dry resting either on the shaped handle of a rolling pin or on a small egg. Make five petals for each tulip. Let the petals dry for several hours before assembling. Adhere the petals together into a tulip shape with a small dab of royal icing. Leave until set. Paint some tulips deep red and some pink with food color. Leave one or two white. Let dry.

**4** Take approximately ¾ cup gelatin icing and color cream to make the freesias. This will make eight freesias. Cut an elongated heart shape from stiff paper. Roll out the icing and cut round the petal template. Gently press the top of the petal between thumb and forefinger to make it as thin as possible. Let it dry over the end of, for example, a pen.

When the second petal is ready, turn the pen slightly. Moisten the edge of the first petal and position the second petal. Continue until there are five petals, and the fifth petal joins the first. Place a small ball of soft gelatin icing in the bottom of each flower and push the artificial stamens into it. Let the freesias dry.

**5** Take approximately 1½ cups gelatin icing and color yellow to make the roses. This will make six roses. With lightly floured hands take a small piece of icing and form it into a slender cone shape. Take another small piece of icing and press it into a semi-circular shape. Moisten the straight edge of the petal and wrap it around the cone to form a bud.

Use a slightly larger piece of icing for each additional petal. Make the petals as thin as possible. Once they are secured in position, gently shape them so that they gradually form an open rose. Work quickly with each petal, because the icing sets rapidly and shaping can become impossible after as little as a minute. Vary the size of the roses and include some buds.

**6** Take approximately ⅓ cup gelatin icing and color leaf green to make the rose leaves. Roll out the icing and cut out leaf shapes with a sharp knife. Quickly score the leaves with a wooden pick to make leaf veins. Let the leaves dry on a curved surface, such as a rolling pin. Paint the leaves with a darker shade of green to make the color more authentic.

**7** Put the cake on the thin cake board. Cut through the board round the edge of the cake with sharp scissors or a scalpel knife. Take the curved piece of wood or cardboard for the handle and wrap gold ribbon around it. Gently press the handle into the marzipan and adhere firmly with small dabs of royal icing. Let set. Place the flowers and leaves in position, attaching each one with a small dab of royal icing. Tie large gold ribbon bows on the handle. For added effect, give the iced basket weave a wash of brown food color. When dry, lightly dust with edible gold luster food color.

# SIMNEL EASTER CAKE

A simnel Easter cake is traditionally made for Easter Sunday. It is baked with a circle of marzipan sandwiched between the two halves of the cake batter.

### INGREDIENTS
1 × 8-inch round fruit cake (see p. 23) baked
   in two halves with marzipan between
about 2 cups Marzipan (see p. 27)
1 egg white, beaten
½ cup apricot glaze

### MATERIALS & DECORATIONS
1 × 10-inch round cake board
crimper
Easter duck (see p. 65) – optional
Gold Ribbon

**1** The cake does not need to be turned upside down, as the top is traditionally slightly domed. If there is a hollow in the top of the cake fill it with marzipan brushed with boiled apricot glaze.

**2** Brush the top of the cake with apricot glaze. Have ready a marzipan circle, cut to fit the top of the cake using the base of the pan as a template, and 12 small marzipan balls. These represent the apostles.

**3** Place the marzipan on top of the cake. Mark across the top of the marzipan with a knife to form a diamond pattern.

**4** Crimp all around the edge. Adhere the marzipan balls in place with a little beaten egg white. The easiest way to position them is 'by the clock', as if you were putting them at twelve, six, three and nine, then filling in the remainder.

**5** Brush the top of the cake and the decorations with beaten egg white. Place the cake under a hot broiler for 30 seconds to brown the surface of the marzipan.

**6** A classic simnel Easter cake does not have marzipan round the sides. Put an Easter duck on top if you like, but it is not traditional.

# EASTER CAKE

This pale yellow iced Easter cake is decorated around the sides and bottom border with piped grass, ducks, rabbits and flowers. In this instance these decorations are made with royal icing, but they could also be made with buttercream, chocolate or praline.

### INGREDIENTS
1 × 8-inch round fruit cake (see p. 23)
about 4⅓ cups Marzipan (see p. 27)
about 3¼ cups Royal Icing (see p. 38)
about 1½ cups Royal Icing for piping

### MATERIALS & DECORATIONS
1 × 10-inch round cake board
pastry bag
tips Nos. 0, 1, 2, 3, 44
shredded coconut
marzipan duck (see p. 65)
Easter eggs (see p. 79)
template (see pp. 196-219)
Food colors: green, yellow, orange, chocolate

1 Marzipan and then ice the cake with royal icing colored pale yellow. Let dry. Pipe around the bottom border of the cake with tip No. 1 and green royal icing.

2 Using the pastry bag end, pipe the bulrush leaves on the side of the cake with light green icing. Then pipe the bulrush heads with tip No. 2 and chocolate icing.

3 Embroider the small flowers on to the side of the cake with tip No. 0 and yellow icing.

4 Pipe a large shell border along the top edge of the cake with tip No. 44. Let dry. Then overpipe a diagonal line across each shell with tip No. 1 and yellow icing. In turn, highlight the overpiped line with delicate green dots. This gives the finished cake a fresh and wholesome feeling of springtime.

5 To create the grass effect on top of the cake, spread a small quantity of royal icing in a thin layer across the center and, before it dries, sprinkle some green colored shredded coconut over the royal icing.

6 Pipe the ducks on the side of the cake using tip No. 2, 3 or 4, depending on the size of the duck. Push out a teardrop shape, curled up at the end. Then pipe a dot for the head and a small bead for the wing on the side. Using a fine tip, No. 1 or 0, pipe the duck's beak and foot with orange icing.

7 The rabbit is piped on the side of the cake with a view of the rabbit's back. First pipe the rabbit's ears with long teardrops, then pipe a bead for the head and a large one for the body. Finally pipe a little white tail on the back of the rabbit.

8 To complete the cake, position marzipan ducks and a basket of eggs on the top.

# THANKSGIVING CORNUCOPIA

This extravagant Cornucopia is designed to celebrate Thanksgiving. If time is limited, you could make fewer fruits and vegetables without losing the overall impact.

### INGREDIENTS
1 × 6-inch square rich fruit cake (see p. 23)
warm apricot jam, mixed with a little water
about 2 cups Marzipan (see p. 27)
about 1¼ cups Fondant Icing (see p. 40)
about 3¼ cups Gelatin Icing (see p. 35)
about ⅓ cup Royal Icing for fixing (see p. 38)

### MATERIALS & DECORATIONS
1 × 12-inch square cake board
wooden pick
fine paintbrush
Food colors: brown, red, orange, green, a variety of colors for the fruit and vegetables, and edible gold luster

**1** Cut the cake in half vertically and assemble the two pieces so that the underside of the two cake halves are together. Stick the two rectangular blocks together with apricot jam.

**2** Cut the block of cake into a horn shape using a sharp knife. Use cut off pieces to make the shape if necessary. Cover with warm apricot jam.

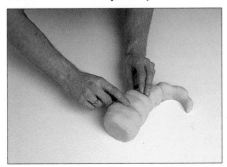

**3** Cut the marzipan into strips approximately 2 inches wide and ½ inch deep. Cover the cake with the strips. Mold the marzipan, forming a ridged surface on the cake by pressing your fingers into the joints between the strips of marzipan. Let dry for 12 hours.

**4** Make approximately 1¼ cups fondant icing and color brown. Roll out the icing and mold it over the cake. Cut away any surplus. Let dry for 12 hours. Paint additional decoration on the horn with brown food coloring. When it is dry, dust the horn lightly with edible gold luster powder.

**5** Make approximately 3¼ cups gelatin icing. Take a piece the size of a tangerine and mold it into a pumpkin shape. Make indentations at the top and bottom. Use a wooden pick to score segments in the side of the pumpkin. Let dry for two hours.

**6** Make a small 'seed' to form the pumpkin stalk. Use red and orange food colors to paint the pumpkin as illustrated. Fix the stalk in position with a dab of royal icing.

**7** To make a cauliflower, take a ball of icing approximately 1 inch in diameter. Use a wooden pick to prick the surface all over with small circles of separate pinpricks to form the florets. Let dry.

**8** Color a small amount of gelatin green and mold into a semicircular piece. Form a frill by pressing into the edge of the icing with a wooden pick. Moisten the bottom of the icing along the edge and wrap around the cauliflower. Continue until there are enough leaves. Let dry for several hours.

**9** To make a cabbage, take ⅓ cup gelatin icing and color green. Roll the icing out into a 3-inch circle. Form a frill by pressing into the edge of the icing all the way around with a wooden pick.

**10** Take hold of the center of the circular piece of icing and fold the frill upwards to form the center of the cabbage. Continue forming new leaves around the developing center, gradually molding the leaves outwards to form a full head of cabbage.

**11** Mold the other fruit and vegetables (see p. 66), and paint them with appropriate food colors, mixing colors where necessary (see p. 62). Make more gelatin icing if you feel you need more fruit and vegetables to create the right effect.

**12** To assemble the cake, place the fruit and vegetables around the rim of the horn, securing the large pieces with small dabs of royal icing.

# FANCY CAKES

Fancy cakes are a traditional feature of afternoon tea. They are generally sponge cake-based and decorated with soft fillings and toppings, in particular buttercream, fondant icing and fresh cream. The decoration is lavish and colorful. Some popular fancy cakes, such as Battenburg and iced petits fours are included here and are definitely for those with a sweet tooth.
If you are new to cake decorating, it is a good idea to start with fancy cakes. The piping techniques involved in the decorations are fairly simple and you can even scrape off the buttercream and start again if things go wrong.

## CHOCOLATE BOX GATEAU

Celebrate a birthday, complete a dinner party or just make anytime a special occasion with this luxurious chocolate gâteau.

### INGREDIENTS
1 × 8-inch square chocolate cake (see p. 16 or 21)
1½ cups Chocolate Buttercream (see pp. 29 and 30)
about ¾ cup chocolate for piping (see p. 80)

### MATERIALS & DECORATIONS
1 × 10-inch square gold cake board
smoother or plain icing comb
chocolate rectangles made ½ inch higher than sides of cake (see p. 80)
pastry bag
tip Nos. 13 and 4
gold ribbon

**1** Make a square chocolate cake and cover it with chocolate buttercream. Put the buttercream on top with a metal spatula and flatten it out. Smooth the sides with a smoother.

**2** Put the cake on its board. Cover the sides with overlapping rectangles of chocolate. They will stick in place as the buttercream dries. The chocolate pieces should be about ½ inch higher than the cake to allow for the decoration on top.

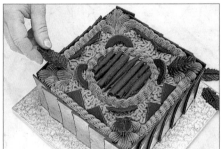

**3** Using tip No. 13 pipe chocolate shells, fleurs de lys and cornelli on top of the cake. Add chocolate curls, triangles and leaves with tip No. 4 as shown on p. 80. Tie a gold bow round the chocolate box to complete the decorations.

# SMALL PETITS FOURS

The ingredients and materials given are sufficient to make 6 of each of the small petits fours illustrated here.

## INGREDIENTS

1 × 9-inch × 6-inch rectangular Genoese
  sponge cake slab (see p. 18)
1 × 6-inch square Genoese sponge cake slab
  colored half pink and half chocolate (see
  p. 143)
½ cup apricot jam
about 1¾ cups Marzipan (see p. 27)
about 2⅓ cups Buttercream (see pp. 29
  and 30)
1¼ cups whipping cream
12 small meringue halves

## MATERIALS & DECORATIONS

pastry bag
tips Nos. 13, 43
chocolate sprinkles
24 chocolate squares (see p. 80)
Food flavoring: chocolate
Food colors: green, pink, chocolate

## PETAL SWIRL

Cut 6 circles from the rectangular Genoese slab, about 1½ inches across. Brush with warm apricot jam. Color generous ½ cup marzipan green and roll it out thinly. Cut four circles for each cake and position them around the cake. Let dry.

Pipe a generous swirl of buttercream or cream on top of each whipped cake with tip No. 13.

## CHOCOLATE ROUNDS

Cut 6 circles from the rectangular Genoese slab, about 1½ inches across.

Flavor ⅔ cup buttercream with chocolate. Coat each cake with the buttercream. Roll the cakes in chocolate sprinkles.

Finally pipe a pink buttercream rosette on top of each cake with tip No. 43.

## CHOCOLATE BOXES

Cut 6×1½ inch square cakes from the rectangular Genoese slab. Brush the sides of each cake with warm apricot jam and position the chocolate squares against the 4 sides of each cake.

Pipe pink buttercream star shapes on the top of each cake with tip No. 43 or 13.

## MERINGUES

The key to successful meringue making is very slow baking.

Pipe lavish swirls of freshly whipped cream onto one half of each meringue and sandwich with the other half.

## NEAPOLITAN PETITS FOURS

Sandwich the chocolate and pink halves of the square Genoese sponge cake with a layer of buttercream. Take generous 1 cup marzipan and roll it out thinly. Brush the marzipan with warm apricot jam. Lay the cake on the surface of the marzipan. Cut the marzipan to the width of the cake and then carefully roll the cake up in the marzipan. Cut the cake into thin slices.

# FONDANT PETITS FOURS

## INGREDIENTS

For 16 petits fours:
1×6-inch square Genoese sponge cake slab
½ cup apricot jam
about 1½ lb Marzipan (optional) (see p. 27)
about 1½ lb Fondant Icing (see p. 40)
about ¾ cup Royal Icing (see p. 38)

## MATERIALS & DECORATIONS

small round and square cutters
pastry bag
tip No. 1
Food flavorings: lemon extract, rose water
Food colors: yellow, pink, and a variety of
    colors for the flowers

These small petits fours are cut from a Genoese slab cake using either round and square cutters or a sharp knife. Each cake is approximately 1½ inches across. The cakes are coated with fondant icing which sets fairly quickly. For a more professional finish, coat them first with the marzipan.

Divide the fondant icing in half. Color one half yellow and flavor it with lemon extract. Color the other half pink and flavor with rose water. Coat the cakes with fondant icing following the instructions on p. 55.

Pipe simple flower designs freehand with colored royal icing and tip No. 1.

# BATTENBURG

Battenburg is a traditional European fancy cake. It is made by wrapping marzipan around oblongs of alternating pink and plain sponge cake.

### INGREDIENTS
2×8-inch×4-inch oblong sponge cakes (see pp. 16, 18 and 21)
¾ cup raspberry or strawberry jam
about 2 cups Marzipan (see p. 27)

### MATERIALS & DECORATIONS
cardboard
wax paper
crimper
powdered sugar for dusting
candied cherries
angelica
Food color: pink

1 You can make a Battenburg from Victoria sponge cake, Madeira cake or Genoese sponge cake. Color half the batter with pink food color then bake each half in a square or oblong pan. Alternatively, use just one pan and separate the batters with a piece of cardboard covered in wax paper down the center of the pan. When the cake is cool, trim off the crust and cut it into neat oblong blocks. Sandwich the pink blocks and the plain ones together with raspberry or strawberry jam.

2 Sandwich each half of the cake together with another layer of jam. Make sure the pink and plain blocks alternate. These are the traditional colors for Battenburg, but you could vary them and use buttercream instead of jam for the filling.

3 Once the block is stuck together, roll out and cut a rectangle of marzipan to fit the width of the cake. Brush the marzipan, rather than the soft cake, with jam and, starting at one of the jam lines in the cake, roll the cake up in the marzipan and trim off the joint to neaten it. This should be hidden on the underside of the cake.

4 Crimp along the top edges for a decorative finish. Cut a thin slice off each end to neaten it. Dust the top of the cake with powdered sugar and decorate with cherries and angelica.

# NEAPOLITAN

A Neapolitan cake is easy to make and provides a colorful centerpiece for any informal occasion. It is best to make a Neapolitan cake the same day, as the buttercream will tend to harden if it is kept.

### INGREDIENTS
3×8-inch×4-inch oblong sponge cakes
about 1½ lb Buttercream (see pp. 29 and 30)
about ⅔ cup Chocolate Buttercream (see p. 29)

### MATERIALS & DECORATIONS
pastry bag
tip No. 13
serrated icing comb
chocolate triangles (see p. 80)
walnut half
Food colors: pink, chocolate

**1** For this cake you need three colors of sponge cake – plain, chocolate and pink. Make the cakes and trim them very carefully with a sharp serrated knife. Never push a knife into a cake to cut it – always use a slight sawing motion to get a neat edge. Sandwich the three slabs of cake together with pink buttercream.

**2** Cover the sides and top of the cake with pink buttercream and feather the sides with a serrated comb as shown on p. 51.

**3** Pipe a line of shells or a rope of chocolate buttercream down the center of the cake, using a large bag and tip No. 13 and flank it with rows of white, chocolate and pink. Cut a thin slice off each end of the cake to neaten it and decorate the top with triangles of chocolate and a walnut half.

# CELEBRATION CAKES

Cakes are traditionally made to celebrate the highlights of family life – christenings, birthdays, engagements, weddings and wedding anniversaries. This section includes the most elaborate and technically demanding cakes – cakes that are often left to the professionals. With plenty of practice in the skills covered in the first half of this course, however, the amateur cake decorator can rival the professional and create a three-tiered wedding cake that would grace any wedding reception.

## BOY'S CHRISTENING CAKE

This design works well with fondant icing and royal icing. Royal icing is illustrated here. The giraffe is a flooding, piped directly on to the cake.

### INGREDIENTS
1 × 8-inch round fruit cake (see p. 22)
2 lb Marzipan (see p. 27)
about 3 lb Royal Icing (see p. 36)
about 8 oz Petal Paste (see p. 72)

### MATERIAL & DECORATIONS
1 × 10-inch round cake board
scriber
pastry bags
tips Nos. 42, 4, 1
stiff paper
fine paintbrush
flower cutter
template (see pp. 196-219)
Food colors: blue, green, pink, purple

**1** Marzipan, then ice the cake with royal icing. Let dry. When the cake is ready to decorate, scribe or trace the design onto the cake and work from the back to the front of the picture. When you are flooding directly on icing, you do not need to pipe an outline first. Remember, the outline is not there to stop the run-out spreading (it will not spread if your icing is the right consistency), but to stop it contracting as it dries. The icing on the cake will hold it in place, so no outline is needed. Flood the ball in sections and work on other parts of the picture that do not touch each other – the mane, the insides of the ears and the giraffe's back leg – at the same time.

**2** Spread the white flooding icing over the scribed outlines of the giraffe with a paintbush as normal. Then touch the bag with the blue icing into the wet white icing to make blue spots.

**3** Finish up by marking the details with a fine paintbrush or fiber tip pen containing edible food color. Do not be heavy-handed with your paintbrush – remove most of the food color from it before you start so that all your brushwork is very delicate.

**4** To decorate the sides of the cake, cut a piece of paper to fit round its circumference. Fold this first into eight thicknesses. Open it out and you have a regular, curved border to fit the cake. Scribe the curves onto the cake. Cut tiny flowers from pink, blue and purple petal paste with a cutter and push them into a piece of foam rubber. Let dry. Attach the flowers into position on the curves with spots of pale green icing. Dot the centers of the flowers and pipe on the leaves using tip No. 1.

# GIRL'S CHRISTENING CAKE

This attractive Christening Cake can be made for either a girl or boy. The cradle and frills are made separately and then attached to the cake

## INGREDIENTS
1 × 8-inch heart-shaped fruit cake (see pp. 22-24)
about 4⅓ cups Marizipan (see p. 27)
about 3¼ cups Fondant Icing (for the cake)
about ¾ cup Fondant Icing (for the cradle)
about 1½ cups Fondant Icing (for the frills)
about ¾ cup Royal Icing (see p. 38)
about 1½ cups Pastillage (see p. 72)
cornstarch and powdered sugar, for dusting

## MATERIALS & DECORATIONS
1 × 10-inch heart-shaped cake board
crimpers Nos. 4, 5
pastry bags
tips Nos. 42, 4, 0
cardboard
plastic baby decoration
scalloped cutter
wooden pick
fine paintbrush
dog bone tool No. 1
tweezers
flower sprays (see p. 107)
12 ribbon loops (see p. 77)
templates (see pp. 196-219)
Food color: pink

This is a heart-shaped cake covered with marzipan and pink fondant icing. To make a pattern for the curved design on the sides of the cake, follow the instructions for the boy's cake on page 144. Crimp the border, using crimper No. 4, then pipe the shells round the base of the cake, using tip No. 42 and royal icing. Finally add the embroidery work in white and pink icing using tip No. 0. Five tiny hearts form each flower in the sprays.

## TO MAKE THE CRADLE

1 Roll out the pastillage thinly. Make cardboard templates for the head and foot of the cradle (which includes the rockers) and base. Use the templates as an outline to cut the same shapes from pastillage with a sharp knife. Let them dry. To form the curved base for the cradle, drape it over a small rolling pin anchored to the counter with a small ball of fondant. The longer side should go across the rolling pin. Decorate the cradle.

2 When the decoration is dry, lay the head of the cradle flat and pipe along one end of the base and position it on the head of the cradle. When this has dried, pipe along the other end and stick the foot in place, making sure that the rockers are lined up. Let dry overnight.

3 Make the bedding – the undersheet, pillow and quilt – from fondant. Crimp on the quilting pattern using crimper No. 5.

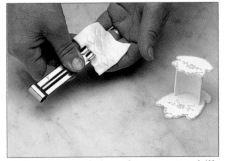

4 Crimp round the edge to get a frill, using crimper No. 4. Put a plastic baby in the cradle and drape the quilt over it. Let dry.

## TO MAKE THE FRILLS

1 Roll the fondant out thinly and cut a circle with a plain or scalloped cutter about 4 inches across. You will need one circle for each scallop of the frill. Cover the pieces you are not using with plastic wrap to stop them drying out.

2 Cut a circle from the center. The width of the ring remaining will be the width of the frill, so use a large inside cutter if you want a shallow frill. On this cake, the lower frill is deeper than the upper one.

3 Lay the ring on the counter with a fine dusting of cornstarch and confectioner's sugar. Position the point of a wooden pick about ¼ inch onto the edge of the ring. Rotate the pick using the index finger of your left hand over the surface of the icing. The edge will pucker up behind the pick as it rolls along the edge. Move the pick to the next section and repeat all the way round the ring.

*continued overleaf*

146

# 18TH BIRTHDAY CAKE

4 Cut the frill. Moisten the cake under the line of the crimped scallop with a fine brush. Paint further than you think you will need, so that you can attach the frill all in one movement. Holding the frill in your left hand, feed it onto the cake with your right hand. Work swiftly to get it into position before it dries. Use your thumb to push it against the side of the cake. If you are using two frills, make the lower one first. It will not matter if it is not perfect, as the top will be obscured by the upper frill. Support the frills with cotton balls until they dry.

Put the second frill as close as possible to the line of crimping and press it into place with the dog bone tool No. 1 or the smooth handle of a teaspoon. If the crimping has been allowed to dry for two or three days, no harm will come to it. Use a paintbrush to lift the frills gently from the sides of the cake when they are nearly dry. Once the frills are thoroughly dry, you can shade them with edible food coloring.

## TO FINISH THE TOP

Place the cradle in position leaving space for any writing you may want to put on the cake. Dampen a small ball of fondant and put it behind the cradle. Using a pair of tweezers, insert about a dozen ribbon loops (see p. 77) into the fondant. Starting from the center back of the cradle add the flower sprays. Secure the cradle with a little royal icing and set the baby and the quilt in place. Pipe a couple of little doves or other motifs, piping the wings and tail separately. Pipe a teardrop shape for the bird's body, attach the wings by pushing them into the teardrop of icing and pipe a bead at the tip of the head, pulling it away to form a beak. Such small decorations as birds are very useful on many cakes to balance the decorations and may also be used to cover a blemish in the icing.

The basic design of this 18th Birthday Cake can easily be adapted to a wedding anniversary cake or an engagement cake, with initials instead of the figures in the center frame.

### INGREDIENTS
1 × 10-inch square fruit cake (see p. 23)
about 4⅓ cups Marzipan (see p. 27)
about 4⅔ cups Royal Icing (see p. 38)

### MATERIALS & DECORATIONS
1 × 12-inch square cake board
scriber
paintbrush
pastry bags
tips Nos. 2, 1, 0, 43
templates (see pp. 196-219)
Food colors: peach, green

1 Marzipan and then ice the cake with royal icing. Let dry. Scribe the numbers on to the cake and then paint in the outline with peach food color. Dilute some green food color with a little water and paint the green fan design inside the number 8. Pipe a double outline around the numbers with royal icing and tip No. 2.

2 Pipe a frame of freehand scroll work around the numbers. Start with the 'C' and 'S' scrolls, using tip No. 2 and peach icing, in the corners, about 1½ inches from the number. Complete the box with scrolls. Overpipe with tip No. 1 and then No. 0. Pipe an inner border of small scrolls with peach icing.

3 Pipe the outer frame of scallops in green icing with tip No. 0. Fill in the area between the scallops and peach scrolls with pale green cornelli (see p. 100).

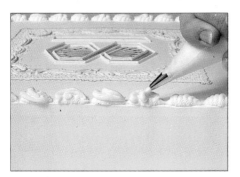

4 Using tip No. 43, pipe a border of oval twisted rope (see p. 99) round the top of the cake and at the base, where it meets the board. Once the ovals are dry on the top edge of the cake, use tip No. 43 to overpipe 'C' and 'S' scrolls.

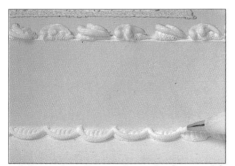

5 Overpipe the ovals at the base with scallops using tip No. 43. Then overpipe with tip No. 2 and No. 1 in white icing and No. 0 in peach icing. Pipe a fine scallop edge on the board. Then overpipe shallow scallops with tip No. 2 and No. 1 and white icing and then No. 0 and peach icing. Finish off the top and base decorations with fine peach overpiping.

# 21ST BIRTHDAY CAKE

The vintage car scene on this key-to-the-door 21st birthday cake could be replaced with an oblong of scroll work if you feel it is too ambitious.

### INGREDIENTS
1 fruit cake (see p. 22 and 23) baked in an 8-inch long key frame (or see Step. 1)
about 2 lb Marzipan (see p. 27)
about 2 lb Fondant Icing (see p. 40)
about 8 oz Royal Icing (see p. 38)

### MATERIALS & DECORATIONS
oblong cake board 2 inches wider than the cake all round
crimper No. 2
fine paintbrush
4 pastry bags
tips Nos. 42, 1, 0
templates (see pp. 196-219)
Food colors: skintone, brown, yellow

**1** To make a key cake, you can either use a key frame or pan or make an oval or round cake for the key head and a square cake for the shank. Cut the square cake into an oblong and use the remaining strip to make the two side pieces. Cover the cake with marzipan and then fondant icing. The fondant is colored skintone, which gives a delicate peachy warmth. Set the cake on the oblong board and crimp the edges.

**2** First paint in the brown scrolls for the sides. Outline the heavier side decorations, then fill them in with dark brown food color. Pipe the shell border at the base of the cake with tip No. 42 and dot it with brown icing, using tip No. 1.

**3** Paint the background scene for the car with brown food coloring and wash it over with a slightly dampened brush. Flood the main sections of the car with yellow and brown icing working as usual from the back to the front.

**4** When the flooded icing is dry, paint in the details of the car with yellow and brown food color and a fine paintbrush.

**5** Flood the numbers with dark brown royal icing and attach to the cake with a small dab of royal icing. Using tip No. 0 and dark brown icing pipe the scroll work on the top of the cake following the scribed design. This can be done all at once, or in sections.

# TRADITIONAL BIRTHDAY CAKE

This traditional birthday cake in royal icing features a very attractive tassel border. Other sprays of flowers as well as the sweet peas are shown on p. 107.

### INGREDIENTS
1 × 10-inch round rich fruit cake (see p. 23)
about 7 cups Marzipan (see p. 27)
about 4⅔ cups Royal Icing (see p. 38)

### MATERIALS & DECORATIONS
1 × 13-inch round cake board
pastry bag
tips Nos. 12, 1, 0, 2 and 4
pink flowers (see p. 76)
sweet peas (see p. 108)
template (see pp. 196-219)
Food colors: pink, green

**1** Marzipan and then ice the cake with royal icing. Let dry. Working with tip No. 12, pipe a star at the base of the cake where it touches the board and pull it up the side of the cake, tailing off the pressure so that the tassel is about 2 inches high. Pipe tassels all the way round the cake.

**2** When they are dry, pipe the loops in pink icing. Using tip No. 1, string a set of loops between the points of alternate tassels. It is important not to pull the tip away too quickly. Keeping constant pressure, let the icing fall out while taking the tip to the point of the next-but-one tassel. Repeat the process with the intervening tassels making each loop longer than the preceding one. The whole pattern is repeated three times.

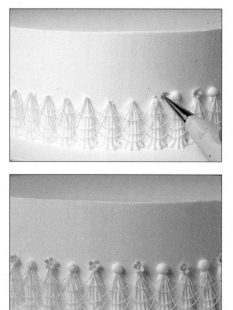

**3** Top the tassels with pink flowers cut with the blossom cutter (see p. 76) alternating with white beads using tip No. 2. Hold the flowers in place with a spot of royal icing. Using tip No. 1 with pink royal icing, pipe little dots in the center of the flowers all the way around the border.

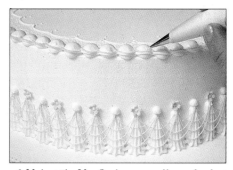

**4** Using tip No. 2 pipe a scalloped edge on the top of the cake. Then pipe the cornelli (see p. 100), using tip No. 0 with royal icing, between the scallop and the edge of the cake. Pipe large beads on the very edge of the cake, using tip No. 4 and overpipe them with royal icing, using tip No. 2. Then overpipe with pink icing using tip No. 1. Then pipe a dot of pink icing at each scallop point.

**5** Pipe the sweet pea stems, using tip No. 1 with green icing, and attach the sweet peas with a spot of royal icing.

**6** Finally you can pipe a name or message beside the spray of sweet peas. Either trace the words on to a paper pattern and scribe them on to the cake and then pipe over the outline, or pipe the words freehand.

# ENGAGEMENT CAKE

The petal-shaped engagement cake is topped with a heart-shaped ring box that would also make a suitable decoration for a wedding cake.

### INGREDIENTS
1 × 10-inch petal-shaped rich fruit cake (see p. 23)
about 3 lb Marzipan (see p. 27)
about 3¼ lb Fondant Icing (see p. 40)
about 8 oz Pastillage (see p. 72)
about 8 oz Royal Icing (see p. 38)

### MATERIALS & DECORATIONS
1 × 12-inch petal-shaped cake board
cardboard
crimper No. 4
tips Nos. 4, 0, 1
wooden pick
tweezers
toy engagement ring
white satin ribbon
templates\(see pp. 196-219)
Food colors: pink, blue

**1** First cover the cake with marzipan and blue fondant icing. Set the cake aside and make the ring case. Make a heart-shaped pattern from cardboard and a fondant mold. The mold should be ¼ inch smaller all round than the cardboard pattern, and about ½ inch thick. Cut out two pieces of white pastillage around the cardboard pattern. Let dry.

**2** Cut a strip of pastillage about ½ inch wide for the sides of the box, stand it on its edge and mold it into a heart shape to fit just inside the base. Let dry. Crimp around the edges of the base.

**3** Dust the fondant mold with cornstarch. Place the heart shape for the lid over the mold and gently shape it down to the edges for a cushioned effect. Use the end of tip No. 4 to cut a series of small circles forming a flower on the lid. Cut circles around the edge. Let the lid, base and sides dry overnight.

**4** To assemble the box, fill the heart frame with pink fondant icing, slightly domed in the center to make a cushion. Attach the frame to the base with a beaded snail trail of royal icing.

**5** While the fondant is still soft, push a toy engagement ring into the cushion. Embroider the sides of the box, using tip No. 0 and pink icing. Then pipe a little border round the cushion with royal icing and tip No. 1.

**6** Using tip No. 0 and royal icing, pipe some filigree work on the inside and outside of the lid. Let dry. Remove the lid from the mold. Fix the lid in place with little dabs of royal icing where the

hinges would be. Prop it open with a wooden pick stuck in a ball of fondant and let dry overnight.

**7** Embroider the sides of the cake, using tip No. 0 or No. 1, copying your design from a paper pattern scribed onto the cake. Then pipe a row of small scallops where the lace is to be attached. Using tip No. 1, pipe a snail trail round the base and add the pink forget-me-nots with tip No. 0.

**8** Fix the ring case in place on top of the cake with a spot of royal icing and put a ball of fondant – moistened with water – behind it. Using fine pointed tweezers, insert the white satin ribbon loops, starting at the center behind the ring case and working all round until the ball of fondant is completely covered.

**9** Add a few sprays of pink pulled flowers, dusted with pink petal dust (see p. 72, No. 5).

**10** The lacework is always put on last because it is so fragile and can easily break if knocked. Pipe the lace onto wax paper, let dry, then remove it carefully with a metal spatula. Pipe a fine line of icing to which you can attach the lace. Pipe it a little at a time – only enough to attach one section of lace – or it will dry before you are ready.

# SINGLE-TIERED WEDDING CAKE

If you do not feel confident enough to attempt a tiered wedding cake, then this simple but elegant single-tiered cake is ideal

### INGREDIENTS
1 × 10-inch square fruit cake (see pp. 22 and 23)
about 7 cups Marzipan (see p. 27)
about 4⅔ cups Royal Icing (see p. 38)

### MATERIALS & DECORATIONS
1 × 14-inch square cake board
tips Nos. 3, 2, 1, 43, 0
pastry bag
wax paper
sugar bells (see p. 78)
twisted white ribbon
template (see pp. 196-219)

**1** Marzipan and then ice the cake with royal icing. Let dry. The design for this cake is very simple – three scallops piped above and below the edge of the cake on all four sides. First, pipe a row with tip No. 3, followed by No. 2. Then pipe another row with tip No. 2 and finally with tip No. 1.

**2** Put a shell edge, using tip No. 43, around the corners with beading down the edges, using tip No. 2, and in towards the center. The beading and scallops are mirrored on the board. The shells at the base and round the corners are underlined with scallops, using tip No. 1. The large scallops are filled with cornelli work, using tip No. 0.

**3** The wedding bells for the sides of this cake are flooded, then the clangers and the scalloped edges are piped. When the bells are dry, adhere them to the cake with royal icing.

**4** The top is decorated with sugar bells attached with a spot of royal icing, and twirled white ribbon.

# TWO-TIERED WEDDING CAKE

This very elaborate looking cake is surprisingly made without a pattern. All you need to do is divide both cakes into eight, and this will give you the basis for your design.

### INGREDIENTS
1×7-inch fruit cake (see pp. 22 and 23)
1×10-inch round fruit cake (see pp. 22 and 23)
about 10 cups Marzipan (see p. 27)
about 7 cups Royal Icing (see p. 38)
about ⅓ cup Fondant Icing (see p. 40)

### MATERIALS & DECORATIONS
1×9-inch round cake board
1×13-inch round base board
wax paper
thin cardboard
pastry bags
tips Nos. 44, 42, 2, 1, 0
polystyrene
6½ft silver lace banding
4×3½ inch pillars
4 wooden skewers
templates (see pp. 194-219)

## TO MAKE THE CORONET

**1** The coronet for the top is made in nine separate sections – eight side panels and an octagon for the base. First cut the paper pattern. Each side panel consists of trellis work and flooding. Flood the octagon for the base and let dry.

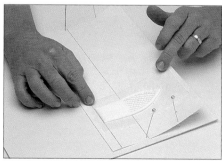

**2** The sides of the crown need to be tilted slightly outwards from the point where the filigree work starts. So mark the base line and a line for the start of the filigree on a piece of thin cardboard. Fold the cardboard along the second line and pin it to a board, supporting the raised edge with cubes of polystyrene. Line the eight side sections of the crown along the cardboard to dry overnight so that you get a uniform tilt.

**3** When the pieces are dry, lay them in place on the base octagon – remember they will not lie flat because of the tilt, so handle them carefully.

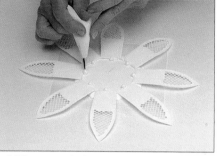

**4** Pipe a circle of icing inside the coronet to hold the sections in place as you lift them up. Pipe a bead at the center base of each section to help hold the side pieces in place as they are lifted.

**5** Supporting each section on a block of polystyrene, lift them gently into place, one at a time starting from the center back, adjusting them and making sure they are supported with the icing.

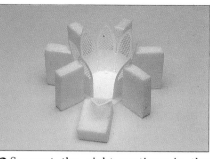

**6** Support the eight sections in the upright position with the polystyrene blocks. The blocks can be cut from a piece of polystyrene packing.

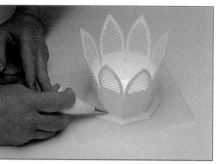

**7** Using tip No. 1 put a beading of royal icing down the joint of each section and round the base, for decoration and added strength.

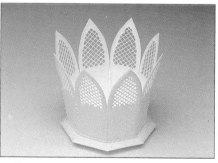

**8** Let the coronet dry overnight. When you are ready to place it on the cake, mount it on a small circle of fondant icing about ¼ inch thick to raise it up slightly. This will make it easier to lift the coronet into place.

*continued overleaf*

## TO DECORATE THE CAKE

1 Marzipan and then ice the cakes with royal icing. Let dry. Divide each cake into eight sections and mark them unobtrusively at the edges. Using tip No. 44 pipe four large shells pointing out from the center of the cake at the quarter marks. Pipe a second set of shells in between the first set at the base board (at the eighth marks). Pipe a tapered row of 'C' scrolls on either side of the shells with tip No. 42. The scrolls at the bottom should come about halfway along the scrolls on the top. The pattern is repeated exactly on the top of the cake and at the base board. But the scrolls finish on the outside edge of the cake top and on the inside edge of the base board.

2 Using tip No. 42 overpipe each large shell with a center line and then pipe a 'C' and 'S' scroll on each side of the center line. Overpipe these when dry using tips Nos. 2 and 1. Pipe three large beads of icing at the tail of the shells, then overpipe them with tip No. 1

3 Let the scroll work dry, then overpipe wtih tip No. 42. Let dry, then overpipe again with tips Nos. 2 and 1. When the overpiping on the C & S scrolls is dry, trellis between them with tip No. 0. Overpipe the scrolls again with tip No. 0. Pipe the scallops, first with tip No. 2, then No. 1. The beading and cornelli work are done with tips Nos. 1 and 0.

4 The graduated dots come directly under the top shells and three more rows rise from the bottom shells. Pipe fine lace work (see p. 101) across the scrolls. Finish the boards by attaching the silver lace banding round the edges of the boards with paper glue or royal icing. Put the pillars in place so that they form a cross between the shells, following the instructions for marking out templates on p. 110 and assembling tiers on p. 113. Secure the coronet in place with a spot of royal icing.

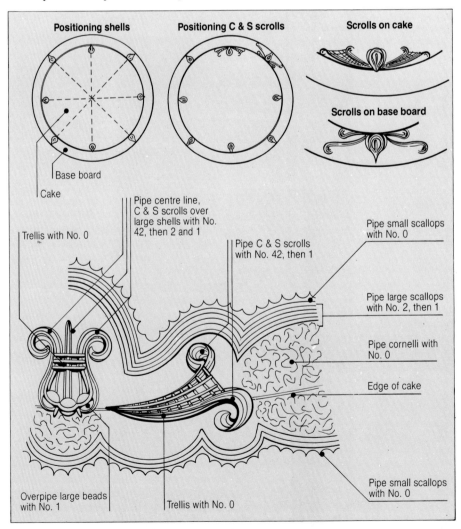

Positioning shells

Positioning C & S scrolls

Scrolls on cake

Base board

Cake

Scrolls on base board

Trellis with No. 0

Pipe centre line, C & S scrolls over large shells with No. 42, then 2 and 1

Pipe C & S scrolls with No. 42, then 1

Pipe small scallops with No. 0

Pipe large scallops with No. 2, then 1

Pipe cornelli with No. 0

Edge of cake

Pipe small scallops with No. 0

Overpipe large beads with No. 1

Trellis with No. 0

# HEXAGONAL WEDDING CAKE

When you are planning a complicated cake like this for a special occasion, bake the cakes two or three months in advance to let the flavor develop, and allow the last month before the celebration to work on the decorations.

## COUNTDOWN

*Four weeks before the wedding:* marzipan the cakes and leave them for a week for the marzipan to harden off.
*Three weeks before:* cover them with fondant icing or royal icing and let them dry for a week.
*Two weeks before:* allow a week for decoration and assembly.

## INGREDIENTS

3 hexagonal rich fruit cakes, 12-inch, 9-inch, 6-inch (see p. 23) (measured point to point)
about 7½ lb Marzipan (see p. 27)
about 12 cups pink Fondant Icing (see p. 40)
Royal Icing for attaching (see p. 38)

## MATERIALS & DECORATIONS

3 hexagonal cake boards, 14-inch, 12-inch, 8-inch
wax paper
scriber
spirit level and ruler
pastry bag and tip Nos. 0, 1, 42
6 wooden skewers
3 × 3½-inch pillars
3 × 3-inch pillars
15 azaleas (see p. 75)
20 flower sprays (see p. 76)
double swan (see p. 105)
9 sets of initials (see p. 216)
ribbon and tulle
silver banding
lace (see p. 101)
templates (see pp. 196-219)

**1** When the fondant on the cake has dried, lay the wax paper on to which you have copied your chosen pattern in position on the cake. Mark the pattern through the paper on to the cake with a scriber. This will give a much finer line than outlining the pattern with pinpricks – even pinpricks will be too large to cover properly with icing from the finer piping tips.

**2** Pipe the shell work at the base of the cake and the outlines for the pattern – the flower stems and curlicues. Fill in with the flowers and leaves. Three sides of the hexagon are decorated with floral motifs and three sides with the couple's initials. The lace work is left until last. When the cake is assembled, the initials alternate with the decorative work. For this cake you will be repeating the design three times, each time on a smaller scale.

**3** Next, prepare to position the pillars on the two larger cakes. On a six-sided cake, three pillars look better than four. (Never try to balance a cake on two!) Work out the position of the pillars on the template according to the instructions on pp. 110-13.

**4** When the pillars are in place, attach the flower sprays, initials and ribbons with small dabs of royal icing.

**5** Insert the azaleas carefully in the flower sprays, attaching each azalea with a small dab of royal icing.

**6** Attach the swans to the top tier. Finally, add the lace work (see p. 101). Do not be tempted to add this earlier in case you knock it as you are completing the other decorations.

**7** Assemble the cake to check the overall effect. Then store each of the tiers in a box. You can buy special wedding cake boxes in sizes up to 18 inches square. The boxes can then be delivered to the reception and assembled on the spot.

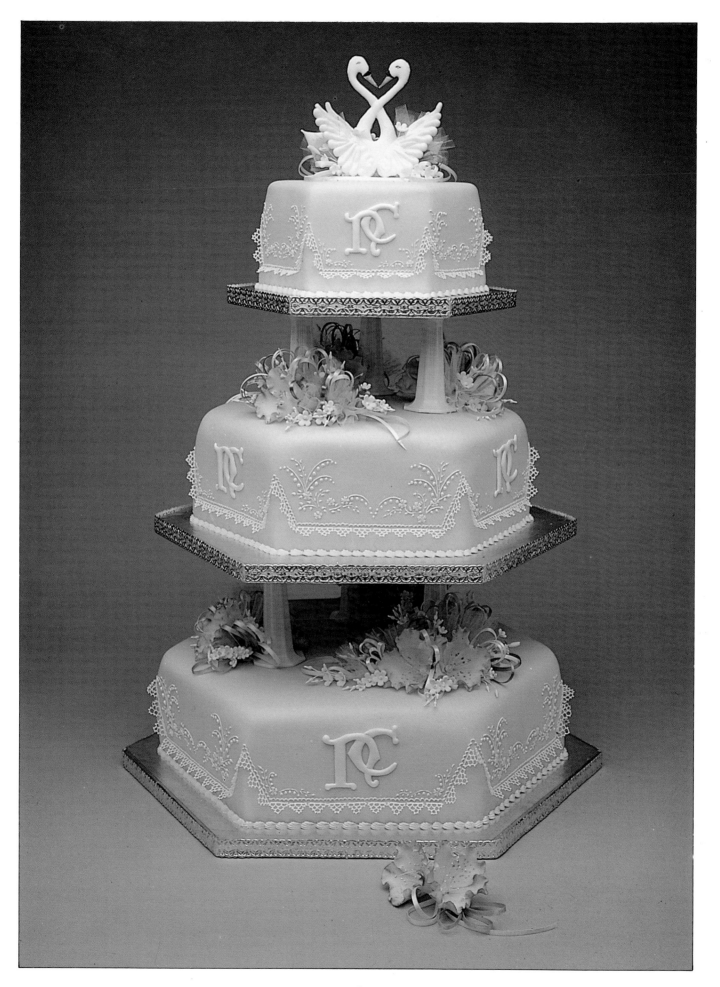

# THREE-TIERED WEDDING CAKE

This very elaborate and professional wedding cake features a royal icing decorative collar and delicate royal icing butterflies.

### INGREDIENTS
1 × 6-inch square rich fruit cake (see p. 23)
1 × 8-inch square rich fruit cake
1 × 10-inch square rich fruit cake
about 6 lb Marzipan (see p. 27)
about 7½ lb Royal Icing (see p. 38)
about 3 oz Fondant Icing for attaching
  (see p. 40)

### MATERIALS & DECORATIONS
1 × 8-inch square cake board
1 × 10-inch square cake board
1 × 16-inch square base board
pastry bags
tips Nos. 1, 0, 2
4 × 3½-inch pillars
4 × 3-inch pillars
12 butterflies (see p. 103)
silver vase, silk flowers and ribbon loops
silver banding
templates (see pp. 194-219)

**1** Marzipan and then ice the cake with royal icing. Let dry. The top collar is made in four separate sections and three-point lace is piped round the edge, using tip No. 0. The bottom collar is flooded directly onto the board using tip No. 1 and then the lace is added using tip No. 0.

**2** Before fitting the top collar you need to mark the position of the pillars. Follow the instructions for making templates on p. 110 and assembling tiers on p. 113.

**3** Pipe the shell border for the first section of the collar (ie from the halfway point on one side, around the corner to the halfway point on the next side). If you pipe the border all around the cake before attaching the collar sections, it will have dried before you finish. Pipe as you go along.

**4** When you have put the collar sections into place, you will find that the collars do not actually meet – the space in between sections is where the butterflies are positioned.

**5** Once all the collar sections are in place, pipe a line inside the edge onto the surface of the cake with tip No. 2. Overpipe with tip No. 1, then pipe another No. 1 line inside the No. 2 line and a No. 0 line to form a graduated effect. Overpipe with a No. 1 line and then a No. 0 to make the border really stand out. Pipe a dab of royal icing in the space between the collars and attach the butterflies.

**6** Put the eight pillars in place ready for the cake to be assembled. The ornament for the top of the cake is a silver vase filled with silk flowers and ribbon loops. Put a ball of fondant in the vase and arrange the flowers. Finish off the cakes with silver banding. Remember when you are assembling a tiered cake to take a good careful look at it from all sides to make sure the tiers are lined up and everything is symmetrical.

# LAYERED WEDDING CAKE

Each tier of this cake is on its own board. The largest tier sits on a traditionally larger board and the others sit on thin boards the same size as the cakes. This helps to distribute the weight of the cakes evenly. When covering the top two cakes, take the fondant right down over the board edges. Lift off the tiers before you cut the cake.

### INGREDIENTS
1 × 6-inch round fruit cake (see pp. 22 and 23)
1 × 8-inch round fruit cake
1 × 10-inch round fruit cake
about 6 lb Marzipan (see p. 27)
about 6 lb Fondant Icing (see p. 40)
about ¾ cup Royal Icing (see p. 38)

### MATERIALS & DECORATIONS
1 × 6-inch round thin cake board
1 × 8-inch round thin cake board
1 × 16-inch round base board
tips Nos. 1, 0, 42
3 wooden skewers
molded roses: 3 buds, 3 rolled buds, 6 medium, 5 large (see p. 70)
14 ready-made gold leaves
Food color: gold

1 Marzipan and fondant ice the cakes in three shades of gold. Let dry. Scribe the curve for the scalloped lines on to the fondant following an embroidery pattern (see p. 206).

2 Using tip No. 1, pipe the scalloped lines first and fill in the rest of the embroidery freehand with tip No. 0. Start with a flower in the center and work outwards in both directions, filling in with forget-me-nots, stems and leaves. Overpipe the scallop so that it stands out well from the cake using tip No. 0.

3 To assemble the cake, drive three wooden skewers into the bottom and middle tiers to give extra support. Cut the skewers off level with the top of the cake. Sit the next tier on top and hold it in place with a dab or two of royal icing. Pipe shell borders round the joints where one cake meets another using tip No. 42.

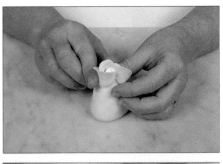

4 To finish the cake, position the molded roses and gold leaves, using royal icing to attach them. Decorate the base board with one medium and two large roses and three gold leaves; the bottom tier with three medium roses and three gold leaves; the middle tier with two medium roses and two gold leaves; and the top tier with three buds, three rolled buds, three large roses and six gold leaves. Place the top-tier arrangement on a small ball of fondant to give it height. Make sure the fondant is invisible when the cake is completed.

# SILVER WEDDING CAKE

The book design of this Silver Wedding Cake could be adapted to any occasion simply by adding an appropriate message in place of the figures.

### INGREDIENTS
2×9-inch×6-inch rectangular rich fruit cake (see p. 23)
about 4½ lb Marzipan (see p. 27)
about 4 lb Fondant Icing (see p. 40)
about 8 oz Royal Icing (see p. 38)

### MATERIALS & DECORATIONS
1×14-inch×12-inch rectangualr cake board
crimper No. 2
plastic ruler or spatula
fine paintbrush
tracing paper
scriber
tip No. 0 or 1
6 briar roses (see p. 74)
length of 1-inch wide green ribbon
templates\(see pp. 196-219)
Food colors: gold, moss green, green

**1** When the two fruit cakes have cooled, turn them out from their pans and place them side by side on a board. Carefully cut a V-shaped section from the center as illustrated in the diagram. Build up two gentle curves to represent the open pages of the book with strips of marzipan. Cover the cake with fondant icing and let dry.

**2** Roll out ½ cup marzipan to ⅛ inch thick and cut into ½ inch strips. Place the strips around the edges of the cake. Crimp the outside edges of the strips with crimper No. 2, to represent the open covers of the book.

**3** Using a plastic ruler or spatula, indent parallel lines along the sides of the book to represent the pages.

**4** Using food color diluted to the consistency of watercolor, paint a leaf design on to the left-hand of the book.

**5** Trace the figures 2 and 5 from the template. Use the tracing to scribe the numbers on to the right-hand page of the book. With No. 0 or 1 and royal icing, carefully pipe the outline.

**6** Flood the outline with royal icing, remembering to brush the icing into position to eliminate any air bubbles and to cover the piped outlines.

**7** Position the briar roses on the leaf design and adhere them with small dabs of royal icing. Attach the green ribbon with a small dab of royal icing. This represents the bookmark and is the finishing touch to the Silver Wedding Cake.

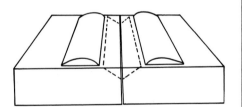

# GOLDEN WEDDING CAKE

This very professional looking cake is decorated without using any piping tips. This makes it ideal for the beginner.

### INGREDIENTS
bell-shaped pan (see pp. 22 and 23 and Step 1)
about 2 lb Marzipan (see p. 27)
about 2 lb Fondant Icing (see p. 40)

### MATERIALS & DECORATIONS
1 × 6-inch round thin cake board
1 × 8-inch round gold base board
1 × 12-inch round gold base board
gold banding
2 frills (see p. 146)
crimper No. 4
flower cutters
ready-made bells and horseshoes
golden ribbon loops (see p. 77)
silk flowers and gold leaves
Food color: gold

**1** The cake is baked in a special bell-shaped pan mold. Alternatively you can use a pudding mold. When you are baking in a pan like this, grease and flour it well and place a circle of paper in the base of the pan. Pack the batter right to the top and bake. Remove pan from oven and if the cake has risen, wait until it has cooled a little and then cut the cake flush with the pan. Turn the cake out of the pan while it is still warm so that it does not stick.

**2** To raise the bell slightly and accentuate its shape, place the cake on a small thin board, the same diameter as the cake. Drape the marzipan and gold colored fondant over the bell while it is on the board.

**3** Place the cake and cake board on the base board. This will allow you to put the frill on more easily. If you cannot get a small cake board to match the base board, adhere a piece of gold banding around the edge of the smaller one.

**4** Make the gold colored frills and attach them to the cake freehand or following scribed lines. Adhere the lower frill first. Brush the line with water and support the frill with your left hand as you stick it on with your right. Be very careful not to flatten the frill as you attach it. Trim the top of the lower frill with a knife to get a neat edge, then adhere the upper frill in place and crimp the edges to make it hold. As the crimping has to be done while the fondant icing is still soft, you can either cover and decorate the cake all in one step, or attach the frill when the covering is dry and finish off the top edge with a border of royal icing.

**5** Crimp two more scalloped borders and make impressions with flower cutters in between (see p. 84).

**6** Attach the bells and horseshoes with royal icing. Make a spray of ribbon loops, silk flowers and gold leaves and use fondant icing moistened with water to attach it to the cake.

# CELEBRATION CAKE

This elegant cake, featuring a collar and decorative side wings, is suitable for any very special occasions – weddings, anniversaries, christenings.

### INGREDIENTS
1 × 8-inch round rich fruit cake (see p. 23)
2 lb Marzipan (see p. 27)
about 2 lb Royal Icing (see p. 38)
about 1 lb Royal Icing for flooding

### MATERIALS & DECORATIONS
1 × 12-inch round cake board
wax paper
tips Nos. 42, 5, 3
templates (see pp. 196-219)

**1** Marzipan and then ice the cake with royal icing. Let dry. When the cake is iced and ready to be decorated, first make the side wings. Measure the height of the cake. Draw out the pattern using the template, adjusting it to the height of your cake. Place a sheet of wax paper over the pattern and fix it with masking tape. Pipe over the top of the design in a snail trail pattern with tip No. 3. Make 4 side wings.

**2** When the wings have dried, release them carefully from the paper with a metal spatula, turn them over and repeat the snail trail on their backs. The wings will be viewed from all sides on the finished cake.

**3** Next make the collar. Measure the diameter of the cake and check it against the collar template. The solid ring of the collar should sit inside the rim of the cake. Draw out the design, secure a sheet of wax paper over it and pipe the outlines. Flood the design with royal icing. When flooding a large solid area like this, select a point from which to begin and work a little at a time from left to right and back again. In this way the icing does not have time to set and leave joint lines.

**4** The top and sides of the cake are divided into 8 sections with lines of beading. Pipe cornelli work (see p. 100) in alternate sections on the top and sides of the cake.

**5** There are 8 piped birds around the cake – one on each side of the cornelli sections. For each bird, first pipe one wing on to wax paper. Pipe an elongated bead of icing on to the side of the cake to form the body of the first bird. Taper the icing at one end to form the tail and pipe a smaller, pointed bead at the other end to form the head and beak. Pipe the inside wing on to the body. When the outer wing is dry, release it from the paper and secure it to the body of the bird with a small line of royal icing.

**6** Where the vertical lines of beading on the sides of the cake meet the cake board, extend the lines to the edge of the board to make triangles. Fill in the triangles with cornelli. work.

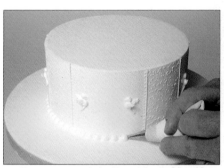

**7** Pipe a row of shells with tip No. 42 or 5 around the base of the cake to conceal the joint with the cake board.

**8** Attach the side wings with discreet lines of royal icing. Finally, pipe a line of royal icing around the top edge of the cake and position the collar.

# FANTASY CAKES

Moving away from the traditional designs of cake decorating, this section lets imagination run riot and uses conventional techniques to create unusual designs. Most of the cakes in this section were designed by Crumbs of London, who specialize in one-off cakes made to order. There is no need to copy these cake designs exactly. Tailor the idea to the occasion or, if it is a birthday, to the person. Each of these fantasy cakes will take between five and ten hours of actual work, excluding drying time. Most of the models have to be left for several hours or overnight to dry before they can be assembled, so start well ahead of time.

## NUMBER TWO

Always bake number or alphabet cakes with the frames upside down, so that you can use the flat base of the cake as the top. Line the frame as for a round pan.

### INGREDIENTS
sponge cake (see pp. 16 and 17) baked in a
   number mold (use amount for an 8-inch
   round cake)
about 1 lb Buttercream (see pp. 29 and 30)
about 2 lb Fondant Icing (see p. 40)
about 8 oz Royal Icing (see p. 38)

### MATERIALS & DECORATIONS
cake board at least 2 inches larger than the
   cake on all sides
tips Nos. 42, 1
wax paper
toys for decoration

### HANDY HINT

If making a cake with two numbers, work with the more difficult one on the board, so as not to move it around, and then put the second number in place after you have decorated the first.

**1** Cut the cake very carefully as shown with a long sharp knife to level its base. Try to cut only a very thin slice from the cake.

**2** Spread the top and sides of the cake thinly with buttercream to coat it and give a good smooth finish on which to lay the icing. Buttercream is preferable to apricot jam. As jam is spread over a soft cake, especially one with an awkward shape, it tends to

encourage crumbs. If it is necessary to remove any excess buttercream, ensure that it does not contain any cake crumbs, as it is to be replaced with the balance of any unused mixture. Place the coated cake in the refrigerator for a few minutes as the chilled air will harden the buttercream and make it easier to cover the cake with the fondant icing.

**3** Drape the cake in blue fondant icing. Mold it into the curves and cut off the excess icing, making sure not to cut off too much from the sides of the cake. Pipe a shell border round the cake.

**4** Pipe a decorative edge round the top and bottom of the cake, add the candles and a present for each year and pipe on the child's name with a fine tip.

# STRAWBERRY

This impressive strawberry is actually quite simple to make. Other fruits can be made in a similar way.

### INGREDIENTS
1 × 2 lb spherical fruit cake (see pp. 22 and 23)
1 lb Almond Paste (see p. 27)
about 1 lb Fondant Icing (see p. 40)
little sherry (optional)

### MATERIALS & DECORATIONS
shell tool No. 2
pastry bag
tip No. 2
template (see pp. 196-219)
Food colors: red, green, yellow

**1** Use a spherical pan to make the cake. Cover it with almond paste, but instead of tucking the paste in and cutting it off at the base, pull it out to form the point of the strawberry. Cover the cake with red fondant icing. Use the back of the shell tool to make indentations in the strawberry.

**2** Cut out a paper pattern for the green strawberry cap and cut around it with a sharp knife on thinly rolled green fondant icing.

**3** Pull away the surrounding fondant so that you do not disturb your shape and lift the shape carefully from the surface with a metal spatula.

**4** Drape the cap over your hand, as it is quite heavy and may tear, and adhere to the back of the strawberry with the aid of a little sherry or water brushed on the strawberry.

**5** Turn up the ends of some of the leaves and make a stalk from some of the excess fondant icing.

**6** With yellow royal icing and tip No. 2, pipe little seeds in the base of each dimple to complete the effect.

# TEDDY BEAR'S PICNIC

This delightful cake makes an ideal centerpiece for a children's party. You can add more or less detail according to the time available.

### INGREDIENTS
1 × 8-inch round rich fruit cake (see p. 23)
warm apricot jam, mixed with a little water
about 12 oz Marzipan (see p. 27)
about 1½ lb Fondant Icing (see p. 40)
about 1 lb Gelatin Icing (see p. 35)
about 4 oz Royal Icing for attaching (see p. 38)

### MATERIALS & DECORATIONS
1 × 10-inch round cake board
wooden pick
small pastry cutter
fine paintbrush
Food colors: blue, green, red, yellow, black, silver

**1** Turn the cake upside down. Spread with warm apricot jam. Roll out the marzipan and cover the cake. Let dry for 12 hours.

**2** Use about ¾ cup fondant icing. Moisten the marzipan on the cake. Roll the fondant out into a circle and mold it over the top and sides of the cake, cutting away any surplus. Let dry for several hours.

**3** Take ⅓ cup gelatin icing and color pale blue. Roll out the icing and cut out an 8-inch square to make the tablecloth. Let dry. Position the cloth on the cake and let dry.

**4** Paint a rough check design on the tablecloth with different food colors. Paint flowers and grasses around the sides of the cake.

**5** Use about ¾ cup gelatin icing. Mold the tea set – cups, saucers, teapot, sugar bowl and spoon, milk jug, knife and plates. A wooden pick is a useful tool for making the smaller pieces.

**6** To make the plates, cut out circles of icing with the small pastry cutter. Give the plates a scalloped edge with the wooden pick before letting them dry. Let each circle dry in the bottom of a wine glass, which will form a lip around the edge of the plate. Mold the large cakes, small cakes and sandwiches.

**7** Decorate the tea set with a fine paintbrush in a blue design. It can be simpler than the one illustrated. Let dry.

**8** Take about 1½ cups fondant icing and color it deep yellow. Mold the separate sections of each bear – body, legs, arms, head, nose and ears – and let dry.

**9** Assemble the three bears with small dabs of royal icing. With a darker yellow, paint in detail of their eyes, mouth, paws and body.

**10** Take about ⅓ cup gelatin icing. Make the stereo head set. Attach the headphones to the bear's head. Paint on the wires using black food color. Paint the stereo black and silver and place it against the side of the bear.

**11** Mold small squares from the remaining gelatin icing, adhere the napkins in position and let dry. Paint each napkin with a bright check design. Assemble the cake.

# WATER LILY AND DRAGONFLY

If you want to keep the lilies after this spectacular cake is cut, just rest them in position while the cake is displayed.

## INGREDIENTS
1×8-inch round rich fruit cake (see p. 23)
warm apricot jam, mixed with a little water
about 1 lb Marzipan (see p. 27)
about 8 oz Fondant Icing (see p. 40)
about 1½ lb Gelatin Icing (see p. 35)
about 8 oz Royal Icing for attaching (see p. 38)

## MATERIALS & DECORATIONS
1×12-inch cake board
stiff paper
Food colors: blue, cream, yellow, green, red, tangerine, orange

**1** Turn the cake upside down. Spread with warm apricot jam and cover with marzipan. Let dry for at least 12 hours.

**2** Take about ¾ cup fondant icing and color pale blue. Roll out the icing into a circle approximately 10 inches in diameter (2 inches larger than the top of the cake). Lay the icing over the cake. Lightly dust your hands with cornstarch and gently mold the icing over the top and sides of the cake. Cut away any surplus. Let dry for 12 hours.

**3** Take 1¼ cups gelatin icing and color pale cream. (This is enough icing to make three lilies.) Using stiff paper, cut out three spear shapes in decreasing sizes (3 inches, 2½ inches, and 2 inches) to represent the petals. Make one petal at a time. Roll out a small piece of the icing thinly. Lay the largest petal shape on the icing and cut round it. Let the icing shape dry on the surface of an upturned bowl. For each lily, make eight large petals. Cut out eight of the medium-sized petal shapes and let dry on a surface with a tighter curve. Cut out six of the smallest petal shapes and

let dry on a still tighter curve.
Cut out a circular piece of icing approximately 2 inches in diameter. Let dry.

**4** Take the largest petals and place a dab of royal icing on the underside of the tip of each one. Arrange the petals in position around the circle of icing, with the tips positioned over the center. Gently place a weight, such as a wine glass, on the tips of the petals pushing the iced points down on to the surface of the circle. Let dry until adhered.

Repeat the process with the medium-sized petals, building inside the first circle of petals. Finally add the smallest petals. Make sure that each layer is dry and adhered in position before adding the next.

**5** Take ⅓ cup gelatin icing and color deep yellow. Roll the icing into a 1-inch wide strip. Cut the icing into matchstick-size pieces. Working quickly with a few strips at a time, take the matchstick shapes and press between thumb and forefinger to make as thin and flat as possible. Let the icing pieces dry.

**6** Draw the shape of a lily pad on a piece of stiff paper. Use ⅓ cup gelatin icing and color leaf green. Roll cut out an icing lily pad. Place the icing lily pad inside a dessert or soup bowl,

letting it dry with the edges curved upwards. Make three lily pads. Let dry.

**7** Paint details on the pads using a deeper shade of leaf green. Paint the fish on the surface of the cake, with reds, yellows and oranges and the ripples with dark blue.

**8** Color a teaspoon of royal icing deep yellow. Place it in the center of the lily. Allow to set for a few minutes and then press the stamens into the icing to fill the center of each of the three flowers.

**9** Take the remaining ⅓ cup gelatin icing, and mold the dragonfly by hand. Let dry. Paint the separate segments in rainbow colors and assemble with a small dab of royal icing. Attach the finished dragonfly to one of the lilies with a dab of royal icing.

# NOAH'S ARK

This cake depicting Noah's Ark makes interesting use of textured icing to represent thatched roof and waves.

### INGREDIENTS
1 × 10-inch square rich fruit cake (see p. 23)
1 × 6-inch square rich fruit cake
warm apricot jam
about 1½ lb Marzipan (see p. 27)
about 5 lb Fondant Icing (see p. 40)
about 2 oz Royal Icing (see p. 40)

### MATERIALS & DECORATIONS
1 × 14-inch square cake board
pastry bag
tip No. 2
wooden pick
stiff paper
fine paintbrush
Food colors: brown, yellow, blue,
    variety of colors for the animals and
    figures

**1** Cut the 10-inch cake into two oblongs measuring 10×5 inches. Place one block on top of the other and cut and shape the hull.

Cut the 6-inch cake into two 6×3 inch oblongs. Cut a piece approximately 4×2½ inches from one oblong to form the house and cut the remaining oblong to cut pieces and position them on the cake board.

**2** Brush the surface of the cake with warm apricot jam. Roll out the marzipan and cover the cake. Let dry for 12 hours.

**3** Take 1½ cups fondant icing and color brown. Using the stiff paper mark the outline of all·the faces of the cake to be iced. Cut out the templates. Roll out the icing and cut round the templatés. Moisten the marzipan with a little water and adhere the icing pieces to it. Let dry for 12 hours.

**4** Take 1½ cups fondant icing, leaving it white. Mold the animal heads and figures – a giraffe, a parrot, an elephant, a lion, a panda, a whale and Noah and his wife – and let dry. Mold the trunk of the palm tree and add detail of the bark by pressing a wooden pick into the icing. Cut out the palm fronds. Use a sharp knife to cut a fringe round the edges of the fronds. Let the fronds dry in the bottom of a small bowl so that they dry curving in two planes.

**5** Paint the animals, palm tree and figures with food colors. Adhere the giraffe into position by cutting out a small square in the roof and attaching the neck with a dab of royal icing.

**6** Take ¾ cup royal icing and color yellow. Fit tip No. 2 and fill a pastry bag with the icing. Ice the roof to resemble thatch.

**7** Using a fine paintbrush and brown food coloring, paint the 'wooden' surfaces of the ark to resemble wood grain.

**8** Take 4½ cups fondant icing and color dark blue. Mold into wave formations around the ark. Position the whale in the waves. Dab the surface of the waves with a small amount of royal icing to form crests.

**9** Attach the animal heads and figures, the palm trunk and individual palm fronds with small dabs of royal icing. Position the parrot on the palm tree.

# CUSTOM CAR

This highly decorated custom car is mounted on a block of wood so that the wheels do not take the weight of the cake

### INGREDIENTS

2×7 inches square Madeira cakes (see p. 21)
about 1¼ cups Buttercream (see pp. 29 and 30)
1 cup raspberry jam
warm apricot jam, mixed with a little water
about 2¼ cups Marzipan (see p. 27)
about 2½ cups Fondant Icing (see p. 40)
about ¾ cup Gelatin Icing (see p. 35)
about ⅓ cup Royal Icing for attaching (see p. 38)

### MATERIALS & DECORATIONS

1×8-inch square thin cake board
stiff paper
string
wooden pick
block of wood, 3½×2½×2 inches
Food colors: yellow, silver, red, orange, black

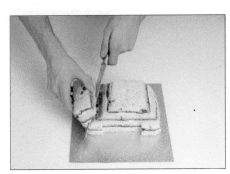

**1** Cut the two cakes in half horizontally. Sandwich the four layers together with the buttercream and raspberry jam. Cover loosely with wax paper and leave for two hours.

With a sharp knife, cut the cake into 7×5-inch rectangle. Cut the cake into the rough shape of the car.

**2** Mark out the exact shape of the top and sides of the cake. Cut out the templates. Spread the cake with warm apricot jam. Roll out the marzipan, cut round the templates and adhere the pieces of marzipan to the cake. Let dry for 12 hours.

**3** Take 1¼ cups fondant icing and color bright yellow. Make new templates for the top and sides of the cake. Remember that the marzipan has added an extra layer to the cake, so the first set of templates cannot be used for the icing. Roll out the icing and cut round the templates. Moisten the marzipan with a little warm water and adhere the icing in position. Let dry for 12 hours.

**4** Take ¾ cup gelatin icing. To make the running board, use a piece of string to measure the length of the cake from front to back including the wheels. Roll out half the icing and cut into a 1-inch wide strip the length of the string. Moisten the marzipan and lay the icing strip the full length of the side of the car. Shape at the front and back. Use the rest of the icing to make the running board on the other side. Let dry. Paint flame designs on the top and sides of the car with red and orange food colors.

**5** Paint the springs and car parts on the back of the car with black and silver food colors. Paint the running boards silver.

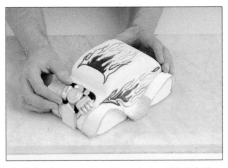

**6** Take ⅔ cup fondant icing. Mold the car parts for the front of the car. Let harden. Adhere the parts in position with small dabs of royal icing. Leave until firmly attached and paint with black and silver.

**7** Put the cake on the thin cake board. Cut through the cake board round the edge of the cake with a sharp knife or scalpel.

**8** Take ⅔ cup fondant icing. Divide it into four pieces and mold the wheels. Use a wooden pick to score the spokes. Let harden. Paint the wheels with black, silver and red food colors. Add red to the running boards.

**9** Take the block of wood and place it underneath the cake. Adhere the wheels to the cake with large dabs of royal icing and let dry.

# JUKEBOX

This unusual Jukebox design is created by building up several layers of sponge cake. The design could easily be adapted to a stereo rack or fruit machine.

---

### INGREDIENTS
3×7 inch square Madeira cakes (see p. 21)
about 1 lb Buttercream (see pp. 29 and 30)
1 lb raspberry jam
warm apricot jam, mixed with a little water
about 1 lb Marzipan (see p. 27)
about 1½ lb Gelatin Icing (see p. 35)
about ⅓ cup Royal Icing for attaching (see p. 38)

---

### MATERIALS & DECORATIONS
1×8-inch square cake board
stiff paper
fine paintbrush
Food colors: blue, silver, black

1 Cut each of the three cakes in half horizontally and again vertically. Stack all the pieces on top of each other, sandwiching each layer with the buttercream and raspberry jam. Cover and leave for two hours.

2 Take a sharp kitchen knife and cut the block of cake into the basic jukebox shape. Place the shaped cake on to the cake board.

3 Mark out the outline of all the faces of the cake on stiff paper. Cut out the shapes. Spread the cake with warm apricot jam. Roll out the marzipan, cut round the templates and adhere the pieces of marzipan on the cake. Let dry for 12 hours.

4 Make new templates for the faces to be iced. Take ¾ cup gelatin icing and color dark blue. Roll out the icing and cut round the templates for the top and sides of the jukebox. Moisten the marzipan with warm water and adhere the icing in position.
Roll out 1¼ cups gelatin icing and cut round the remaining templates. Adhere the icing pieces to the cake. Let dry for 12 hours.

5 Paint a star burst on the front of the jukebox using silver and blue food colors. A cheap paintbrush from any stationery store is ideal for this purpose.

6 Decorate the back of the record deck with silver stars and planets against a dark blue sky background, using the same colors.

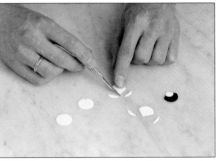

7 Roll out the remaining ⅓ cup gelatin icing. With a scalpel or sharp kitchen knife, cut out small circles to represent the records.

8 Paint the records black with food color and attach in a semicircular arrangement with small dabs of royal icing. Mold the record arm and paint silver. Adhere in position with royal icing.

9 Add a star burst to the front of the jukebox, musical instruments around the top and sides and detail of the record selections with silver food color

# SKIER

The basic idea for this cake can be adapted to any sport – a golfer, a footballer or a swimmer diving off the top board would work just as well.

### INGREDIENTS
1 × 10-inch square Madeira cake (see p. 21)
about 1¼ cups Buttercream (see pp. 29 and 35)
¾ cup raspberry jam
warm apricot jam, mixed with a little water
about 3½ cups Marzipan (see p. 27)
about 3¼ cups Fondant Icing (see p. 40)

### MATERIALS & DECORATIONS
1 × 12-inch square cake board
tracing or wax paper
fine paintbrush
Food colors: red, pink or flesh, blue, yellow, orange, silver

**1** Cut the cake in half horizontally and sandwich together with buttercream and raspberry jam. Cover the cake loosely and let stand for two or three hours. This will make cutting out the shapes much easier.

**2** Choose a sporting figure from a book or magazine, like the skier chosen here. Draw and cut out two separate outlines of the figure on tracing or wax paper. On one of the outlines include details of the main features, such as the head with helmet and goggles, gloves, boots, skis and color flashes.

**3** Take the simple outline and place it on top of the cake. Use a sharp knife to cut round the outline of the skier. Keep the spare pieces of cake and cut into two roughly triangular pieces for the mountain peaks. Spread the cake surfaces with the warm apricot jam. Roll out the marzipan and cover the cake. Let dry for 12 hours.

**4** Make 1½ cups fondant icing. Measure the depth of the sides of the cake. Roll out the icing and cut into strips of the same width. Moisten the marzipan on the sides of the cake and adhere the icing strips in position. Roll out more icing and lay it over the top of the triangular pieces. Usig a sharp knife, cut to the edge of the cake.

**5** Take the second outline of the skier and cut into separate sections, for example the head, skis, gloves, boots and ski suit. Take a small piece of the remaining fondant icing and color bright red. Roll out the icing and cut around the shape of the ski suit. Place on top of the cake. Color a small piece of icing with pink or flesh food coloring and cut round the shape of the head, including the helmet and goggles. Place the head shape on top of the cake, ensuring that the head and ski suit fit exactly together. If the edges do not fit exactly, dip your finger in cornstarch and gently massage the two shapes towards each other. The newly-made icing should remain elastic and easy to work with for some time.

**6** Cut out the skis and place in position. Color a piece of icing deep blue and cut out the gloves and boots. Position on the figure. Using the rest of the blue icing, cut out the helmet and goggles and put in position.
Finally color the remaining icing yellow and orange and cut out the flashes to decorate the ski suit.
The technique is to build up the

figure with layers of icing, ensuring that each piece fits exactly.

**7** Use food colors to paint on the details of the mouth, nose, goggles, legs, knees, boot straps and so on. Paint the skis silver.

**8** Make 1½ cups fondant icing and color sky blue. Roll out the icing and lay it over the cake board. Place the skier in position in the center.

**9** Place the separate pieces of cake on the board. Use blue food color to paint zig-zags on the mountains.

# PEACOCK

This stunning peacock can be set either on a plain silver cake board or on a board covered with green satin.

### INGREDIENTS
1 × 9-inch round rich fruit cake (see p. 23)
warm apricot jam, mixed with a little water
about 1¼ lb Marzipan (see p. 27)
about 12 oz Fondant Icing (see p. 40)
about 2 lb Gelatin Icing (see p. 35)
about ⅓ cup Royal Icing for attaching (see p. 38)

### MATERIALS & DECORATIONS
1 × 10-inch round thin cake board
stiff paper
blue and green ribbon
Food colors: gold, green and blue

1 With a small sharp knife cut out thin scallops around the edge of the cake. Make templates of the top and sides of the cake with stiff paper. Roll out the marzipan and cut round the templates. Spread the cake with warm apricot jam. Adhere the pieces of marzipan to the cake. Let dry for 12 hours.

2 Make another set of templates of the top and sides of the cake. Take ⅔ cup fondant icing and roll it out into a circle. Cut round the template of the top of the cake. Moisten the marzipan with a little water and adhere the icing in position. Take the remaining ⅔ cup fondant icing and do the same with the sides of the cake. The side icing can be attached in several sections and the pieces gently joined by pressing the edges together.

At this point you can either decorate directly onto the fondant icing surface, omitting Step 3 and going on to Step 4, or you can make a gelatin frill as described in Step 3.

3 Draw the tail shape on stiff paper so that the edge extends 1 inch beyond the edge of the cake. Cut out the shape. Cut a second pattern exactly the same shape from stiff card. Using the card shape, make cuts along the top edge 1 inch deep towards the center of the shape, at ½ inch intervals. Do the same along the bottom edge of the pattern. Bend the top edge of the tail upwards and the bottom edge downwards. Take ¾ cup gelatin icing and roll out thinly. Cut around the pattern. Place the icing on the card pattern to dry. Remove the icing from the card. Adhere the icing tail to the cake with small dabs of royal icing. The decorations described in Steps 4 to 7 can either be attached to the fondant icing surface of the cake or the gelatin icing frill.

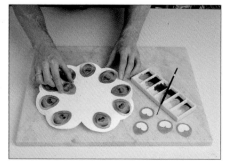

4 Cut two templates for the 'eyes' of the tail from stiff paper, the larger one roughly 2 inches long and the smaller one 1½ inches long. Take ¾ cup gelatin icing. Roll it out thinly and cut round the templates. Make nine large eyes and five small ones. If you have made the frill, let the eyes dry in position on the frill so that they curve correctly. Decorate the eyes with gold, green and blue.

5 Take 1½ cups gelatin icing and mold the body and head of the peacock. Let dry for 12 hours. Paint the body with green, blue and gold food colors, marking in the feathers. Paint in the eyes and beak.

6 Water down the blue and green food colors to make a paler shade. Use the paler shades, together with the gold, to paint in the feathers around the eyes of the tail. Let dry for several hours.

7 Adhere the tail eyes and peacock body in position with small dabs of royal icing. Decorate the sides of the cake with blue and green ribbon.

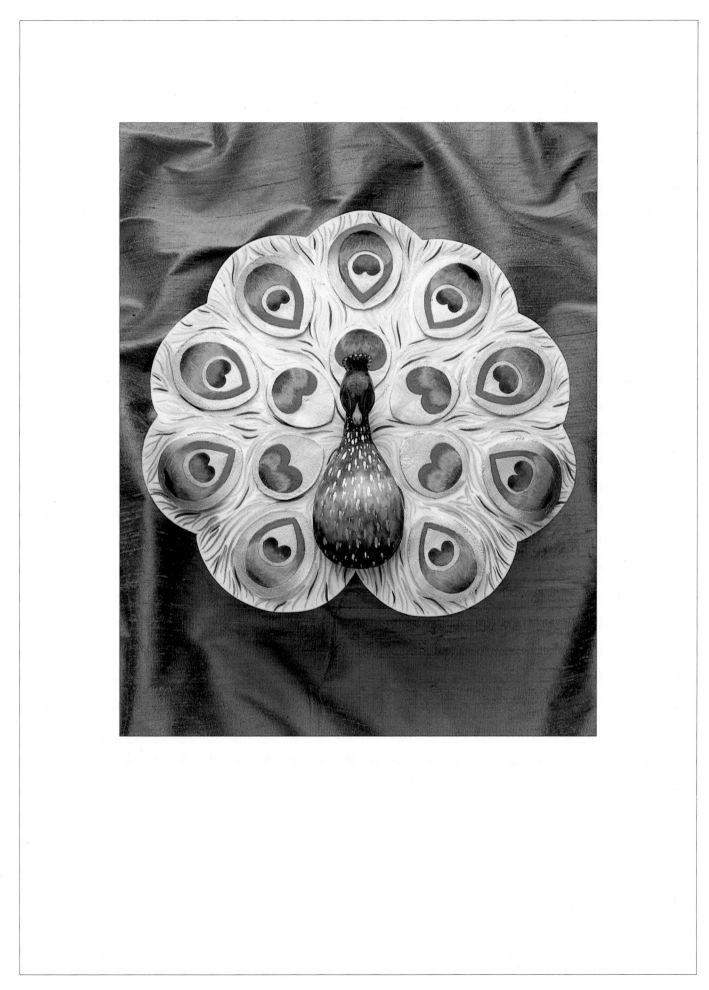

# SPACE SHIP

This fantastic space ship involves quite a lot of modeling and painting with food colors. It is much easier to make than it looks, and only takes about five hours to decorate, excluding drying time.

## INGREDIENTS

1×8-inch square Madeira cake (see p. 21)
½ cup raspberry jam for filling
about ¾ cup Buttercream for filling (see pp. 29, 30)
warm apricot jam, mixed with a little water
about 1 lb Marzipan (see p. 27)
about 2 lb Fondant Icing (see p. 40)
about 1½ cups Gelatin Icing (see p. 35)
cornstarch for dusting
about ⅓ cup Royal Icing for attaching

## MATERIALS & DECORATION

1×14-inch square cake board
stiff paper
plastic egg box
shallow muffin tins
fine paintbrush
Food colors: blue, licorice, green, pink, silver, gold and a variety of colors for the space ship designs

**1** Cut the cake in half horizontally and sandwich the two halves together with the jam and buttercream. Cut the cake again into two oblongs measuring 8 inches×4 inches and sandwich together with jam and buttercream. Leave covered for two to three hours. Cut the cake into a roughly triangular shape, making sure that it slopes down towards the point, which will give an impression of perspective to the finished cake.

**2** Spread warm apricot jam over the surface of the cake. Roll out the marzipan and cover the cake. Let dry for 12 hours.

**3** Using stiff paper, mark out templates of the individual faces of the cake to be iced. Take ⅓ cup fondant icing and roll it out thinly. Cut round the templates. Moisten the marzipan with water and adhere the icing pieces to the cake. Let dry for 12 hours.

**4** Take ⅓ cup gelatin icing. Mark out and cut out a wing shape on a piece

of stiff paper, adding a ½ inch flap along the side of the wing to be attached to the cake. Roll out the icing and cut out the wing shape. Let the piece dry with the 'flap' at an angle of 90 degrees to the wing, for example bent over the edge of a marble slab. Take another ⅓ cup gelatin icing and make a second wing, remembering to turn the template over before cutting. Cut out a tail fin for the spaceship in the same way.

**5** Take ⅔ cup gelatin icing and divide it into three pieces, each the size of a walnut. Take one piece in the palm of your hand and press your thumb into the icing to form a rough cup shape. Take a clean plastic egg box and lightly dust three of the compartments with cornstarch. Try to find a box where the compartments have an interesting shape. Drop the cup shapes into the floured compartments and gently work the icing into the base and up the sides until it reaches the top. Cut off any surplus icing. Let dry. When the icing is quite solid, turn the box upside down and lightly tap on the bottom. The icing pieces will fall out. They will form the rockets at the back of the spaceship.

**6** Take 3 tablespoons gelatin icing and roll it out. Cut out three circles of icing with the pastry cutter for the sounding dishes. Let them dry in shallow muffin pans.

*continued overleaf*

**7** Take about 1½ cups fondant icing and color dark blue. Add some licorice color to produce a deeper color. Roll out the icing and cover the cake board.

**8** Take ⅔ cup fondant icing and add some blue food color. Work this very briefly into the icing and then add another shade of either blue or green. Work these two colors into the icing, but do not blend them in completely. Roll out the icing which will be full of swirls of color. Using a plate or a round cake board as a guide, cut out a quarter circle of icing and place it over one corner of the cake board to represent a planet.

**9** Take 3 tablespoons fondant icing and create the same swirling effect with pink coloring. Cut out a small circle to represent a planet further in space. For additional detail, add rings to this planet using a little gelatin icing and a piece of stiff paper as a guide.

**10** Using the fine paintbrush and silver coloring, mark star formations on the board.

**11** With a variety of food colors, paint designs on the main body of the spaceship. Do the same on the wings and tail fin. Attach the wings to the main body of the cake using royal icing spread liberally along the flaps. Support the wings if necessary until they have dried in position. Attach the tail fin in the same way.

**12** Paint the sounding dishes gold and attach them to each other with royal icing in a triangular formation. Position them on the cake in front of the tail fin and secure with royal icing. Spread royal icing on the flat end of the rockets and place in position, supporting them while they dry if necessary. Position the assembled rocket on the decorated board at an angle, as if it were heading into outer space.

# CAKE DECORATING SCHEDULES

This chart is included to give you a rough idea of how far in advance to begin decorating your chosen cake, once you have some practical experience. The starting point is when you marzipan the cake and takes account of drying time between steps – for cakes involving a lot of modeling, drying time between making the components and assembly will be at least 12 hours or overnight. The number of hours' work given for each cake is a rough guide – it will depend on how fast you work.

The times given assume that the cake has already been made. A fruit cake can be made and stored for a number of weeks before decoration if necessary (see p. 15). It should be made at least 2 or 3 days before decoration to allow the cake to settle. A sponge cake should be as fresh as possible, and is best made the day before you start, giving it time to cool and settle.

| | When to start* | No of hours' work** |
|---|---|---|
| **FESTIVE CAKES** | | |
| Candied Christmas Ring (p. 116) | 2 days ahead | ½ hour |
| Simple Christmas Cake (p. 118) | 3 days ahead | 1½ hours |
| Elaborate Christmas Cake (p. 120) | 1 week ahead | 3 hours |
| Christmas Pudding Cake (p. 122) | 2 days ahead | 1½ hours |
| Star Cake (p. 124) | 2 days ahead | 3 hours |
| Valentine Cake (p. 126) | 2 days ahead | 3 hours |
| Mother's Day Cake (p. 128) | 2 days ahead | 6 hours |
| Simnel Easter Cake (p. 130) | 1 day ahead | 1 hour |
| Easter Cake (p. 132) | 1 week ahead | 3 hours |
| Thanksgiving Cornucopia (p. 134) | 3 days ahead | 8 hours |
| **FANCY CAKES** | | |
| Chocolate Box Gâteau (p. 136) | 1 day ahead | 2 hours |
| Small Petits Fours | same day | 2 hours |
| Fondant Petits Fours | same day | 2 hours |
| Battenburg (p. 142) | same day | ½ hour |
| Neapolitan (p. 143) | same day | ½ hour |
| **FAMILY CELEBRATION CAKES** | | |
| Boy's Christening Cake (p. 144) | 1 week ahead | 3 hours |
| Girl's Christening Cake (p. 146) | 3 days ahead | 3½ hours |
| 18th Birthday Cake (p. 148) | 1 week ahead | 4 hours |
| 21st Birthday Cake (p. 150) | 1 week ahead | 3 hours |
| Traditional Birthday Cake (p. 152) | 1 week ahead | 4 hours |
| Engagement Cake (p. 154) | 3 days ahead | 5 hours |
| Single-Tiered Wedding Cake (p. 156) | 1 week ahead | 3½ hours |
| Two-Tiered Wedding Cake (p. 157) | 2-3 weeks ahead | 7 hours |
| Hexagonal Wedding Cake (p. 160) | 2-3 weeks ahead | 14 hours |
| Three-Tiered Wedding Cake (p. 162) | 2-3 weeks ahead | 14 hours |
| Layered Wedding Cake (p. 164) | 1 week ahead | 4 hours |
| Silver Wedding Cake (p. 166) | 1 week ahead | 2 hours |
| Golden Wedding Cake (p. 168) | 1 day ahead | 2 hours |
| Celebration Cake (p. 170) | 1 week ahead | 3 hours |
| **FANTASY CAKES** | | |
| Number Two (p. 172) | same day | 1 hour |
| Strawberry (p. 174) | 1 day ahead | 1 hour |
| Teddy Bear's Picnic (p. 176) | 2 days ahead | 6 hours |
| Water Lily and Dragonfly (p. 178) | 2 days ahead | 6 hours |
| Noah's Ark (p. 180) | 2 days ahead | 6 hours |
| Custom Car (p. 182) | 2 days ahead | 5 hours |
| Jukebox (p. 184) | 2 days ahead | 5 hours |
| Skier (p. 186) | 1 day ahead | 4 hours |
| Peacock (p. 188) | 2 days ahead | 6 hours |
| Space Ship (p. 190) | 2 days ahead | 5 hours |

\* This information takes account of drying time between steps.
\*\* This figure is a rough estimate – it depends on how fast you work.

# CUTTING THE CAKE

Wedding cake is traditionally served in 1 inch square pieces, or $2\frac{1}{2}$ inch slices. The information in this table will help you calculate what size cake to make based on the number of guests invited. Do not forget extra pieces to send to absent friends and relatives.

There is much less wastage if a cake is cut in slices as illustrated, rather than in wedges.

| SIZE OF CAKE | No OF SLICES (fruit cake) | No OF SLICES (sponge cake) |
|---|---|---|
| 5 inch round | 14 | 7 |
| 5 inch square | 16 | 8 |
| 6 inch round | 22 | 11 |
| 6 inch square | 27 | 14 |
| 7 inch round | 30 | 15 |
| 7 inch square | 40 | 20 |
| 8 inch round | 40 | 20 |
| 8 inch square | 54 | 27 |
| 9 inch round | 54 | 27 |
| 9 inch square | 70 | 35 |
| 10 inch round | 68 | 34 |
| 10 inch square | 90 | 45 |
| 11 inch round | 86 | 43 |
| 11 inch square | 112 | 56 |
| 12 inch round | 100 | 50 |
| 12 inch square | 134 | 67 |

# TIP CONVERSIONS

| BEKENAL* | WILTON |
|---|---|
| **Plain Round** 00, 0, 1, 2, 3, 4 | **Round** 000, 00, 0, 1″ (long tips) 2 to 9 (intermediate round) |
| **Rope** 42, 43, 44, 52 | **Stellar** 501, 502, 504, 172 |
| **Star** 5, 7, 9, 11, 12, 13, 15 | **Open Star** 13 to 35 |
| **Petal** 57, 58, 59 | **Rose and Petal** 362, 363, or 101, 102, 103 |
| **Basket** 22 | **Basket and Ribbon** 47, 48, 49 |
| **Forget-me-not** 37 | **Drop Flower** 224, 225, or 108, 109 |

* Bekenal tips are used throughout the book and are considered amongst cake decorators to be about the best in the world. This chart contains the Wilton equivalents – some correspond exactly but for others there are no exact substitutes. (See pp. 86 and 87.)

# TEMPLATES

This section contains a series of actual-size patterns that are used in the cake designs in Section Two. Below are general notes on making and using templates.

## DRAWING TEMPLATES

To get the best results, draw or trace the design on to tracing paper and use this as a guide to mark the pattern on the cake. This pattern is known as the template. You can either trace off the designs included in this section, find others in magazines or books or draw your own freehand.

## SYMMETRICAL TEMPLATES

Most cake designs are geometric and must be carefully measured and worked out as any unevenness will show up in the finally assembled cake.

1 To make a symmetrical template, cut a piece of tracing paper to the exact size of the top of the cake. Fold the paper into sections of either four, six or eight.

2 Draw a quarter, sixth or eighth of the design on to the top section. Cut out the design using sharp scissors. Open out the paper and you will see the full effect of the design.

## USING TEMPLATES

1 If the same pattern is to be used several times, it is a good idea to copy the design on to a piece of thin card or light plastic.

2 Position the template on the cake and use a fine skewer or scriber to score the outline of the design. Remove the template and pipe along the lines of the pattern, ensuring that the icing covers the score marks. Once the basic pattern is piped, any further icing which is added to build up the design can be done freehand.

ELABORATE CHRISTMAS CAKE (p. 120)

*actual size**

*this is the size used on the cake in
Section Two. You may wish to use a
smaller or larger size depending on
your cake design or use the same
motif in different sizes.

VALENTINE CAKE (p. 126)

*actual size*

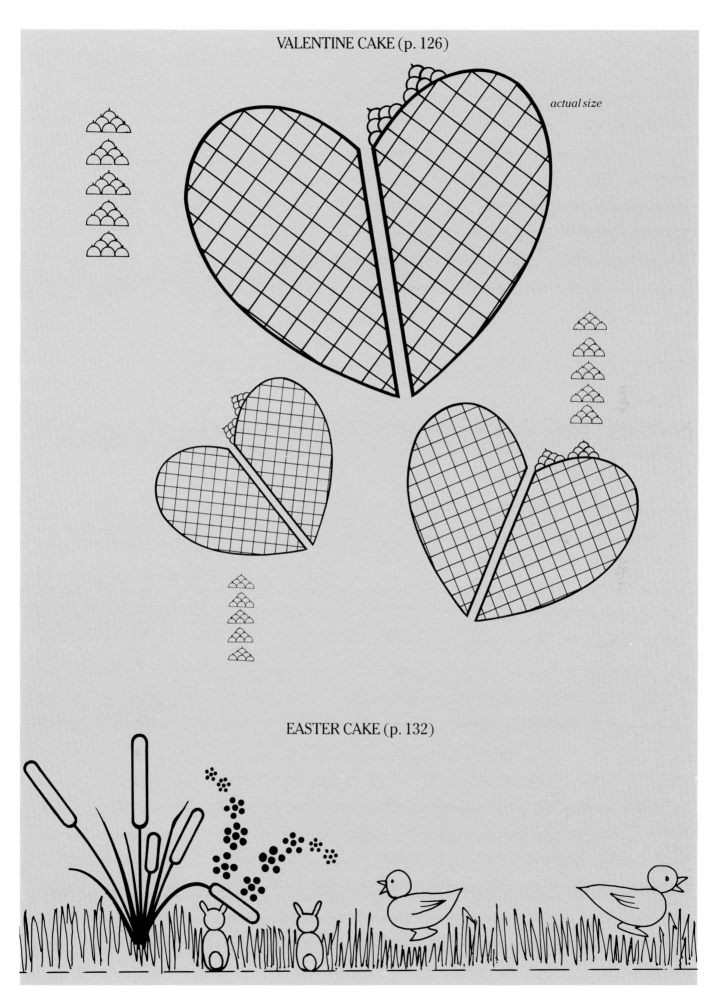

EASTER CAKE (p. 132)

## BOY'S CHRISTENING CAKE (p. 144)

*actual size*

## GIRL'S CHRISTENING CAKE (p. 146)

# ENGAGEMENT CAKE (p. 154)

ring case mold

ring case lid

ring case base

21ST BIRTHDAY CAKE (p. 150)

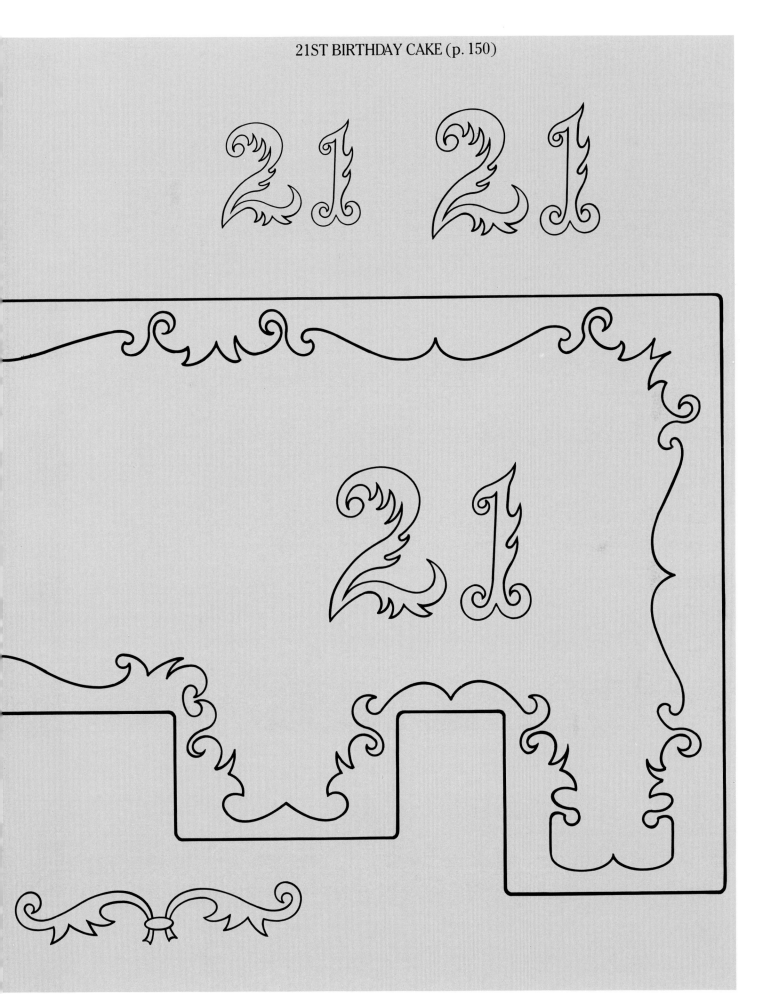

SINGLE-TIERED WEDDING CAKE (p. 156)

*actual size*

TWO-TIERED WEDDING CAKE (p. 157)

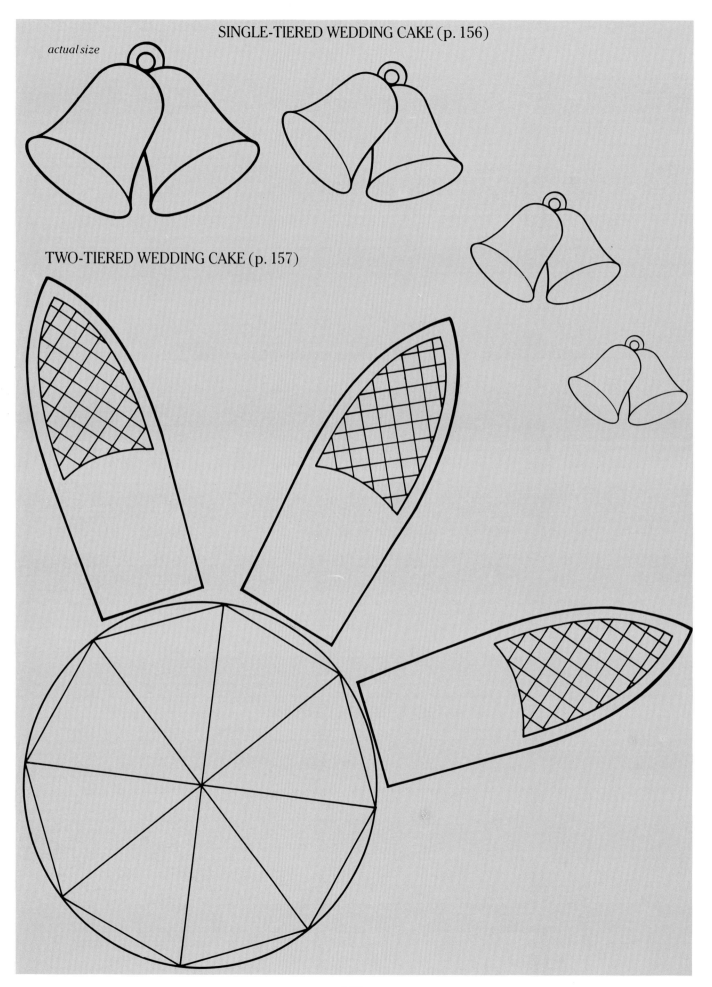

## THREE-TIERED WEDDING CAKE (p. 162)

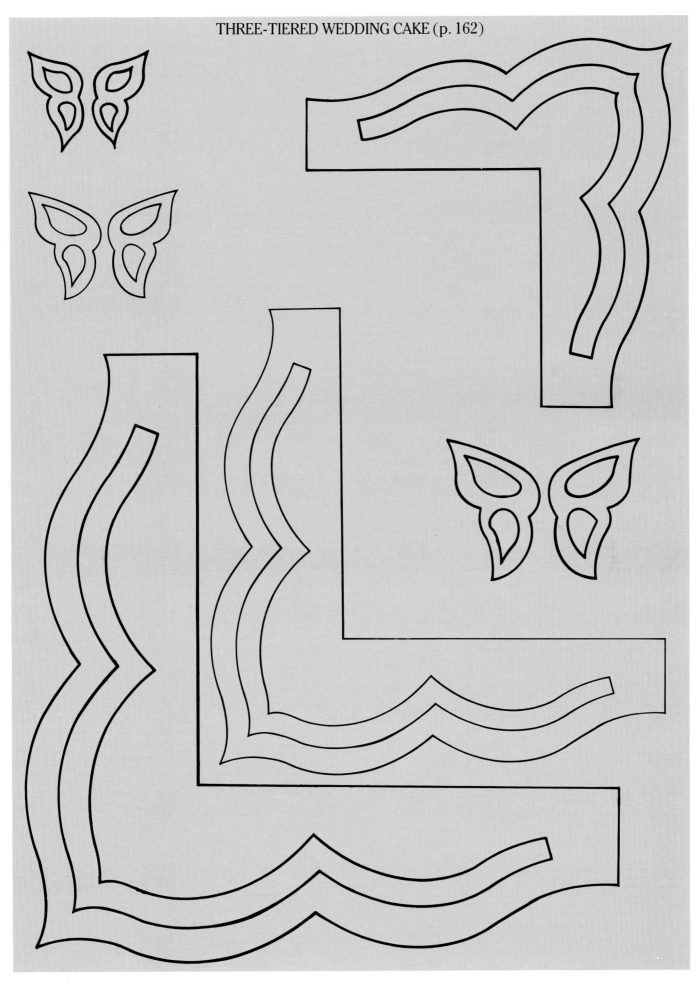

THREE-TIERED WEDDING CAKE (p. 162)

## HEXAGONAL WEDDING CAKE (p. 160)

*actual size*

SILVER WEDDING CAKE (p. 160)

LAYERED WEDDING CAKE (p. 164)

*actual size*

CELEBRATION CAKE (p. 170)

STRAWBERRY (p. 174)

*actual size*

STRAWBERRY (p. 174)

# RUN-OUTS

EMBROIDERY PATTERNS

# LACE PATTERNS

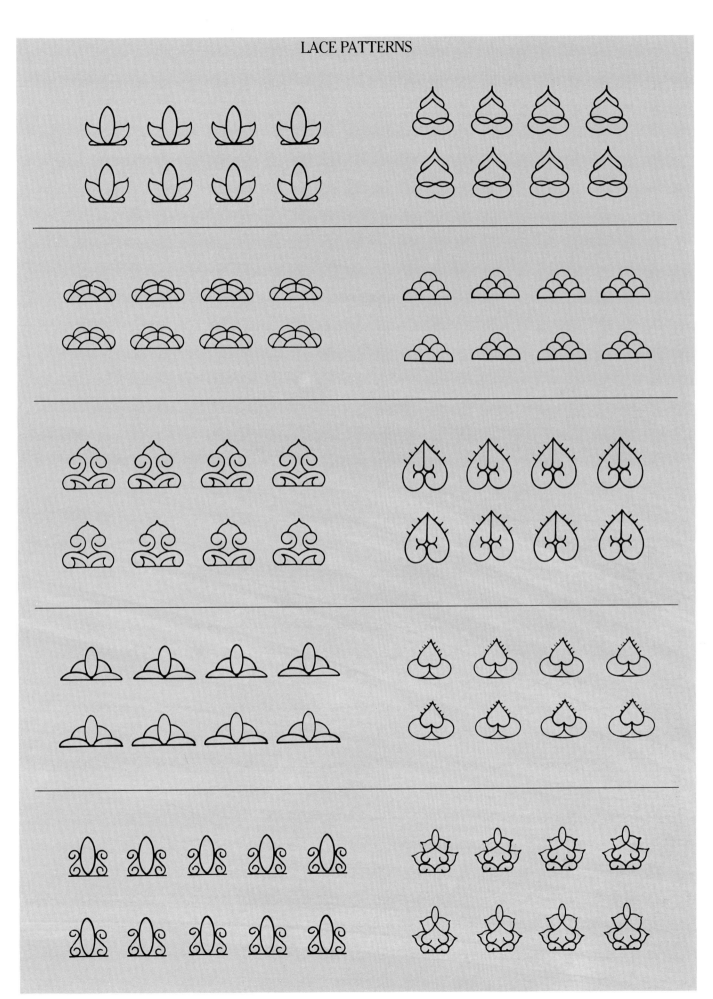

# NUMERALS

## ALPHABETS

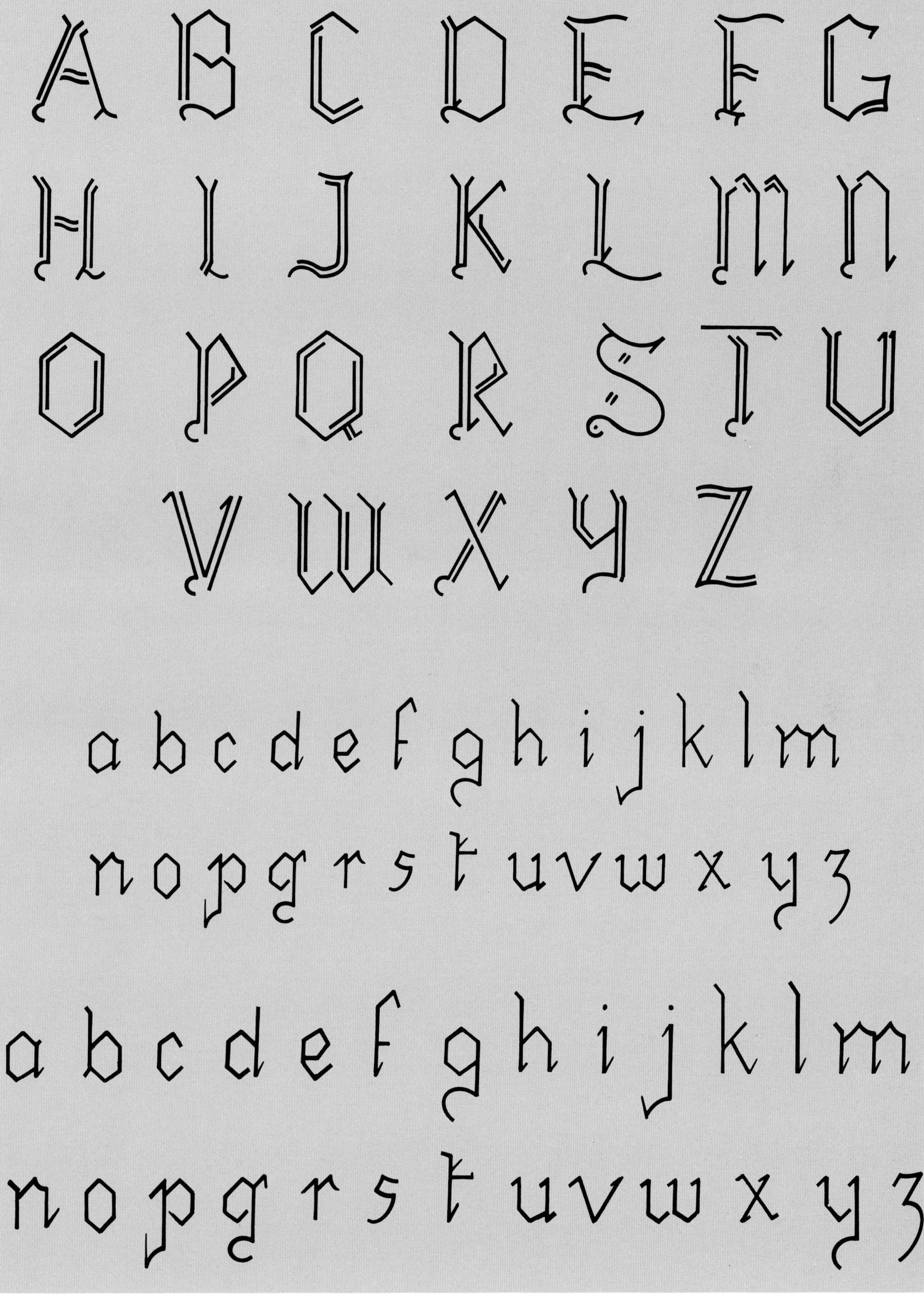

A B C D E F G

H I J K L M N

O P Q R S T U

V W X Y Z

a b c d e f g h i j k l m

n o p q r s t u v w x y z

a b c d e f g h i j k l m

n o p q r s t u v w x y z

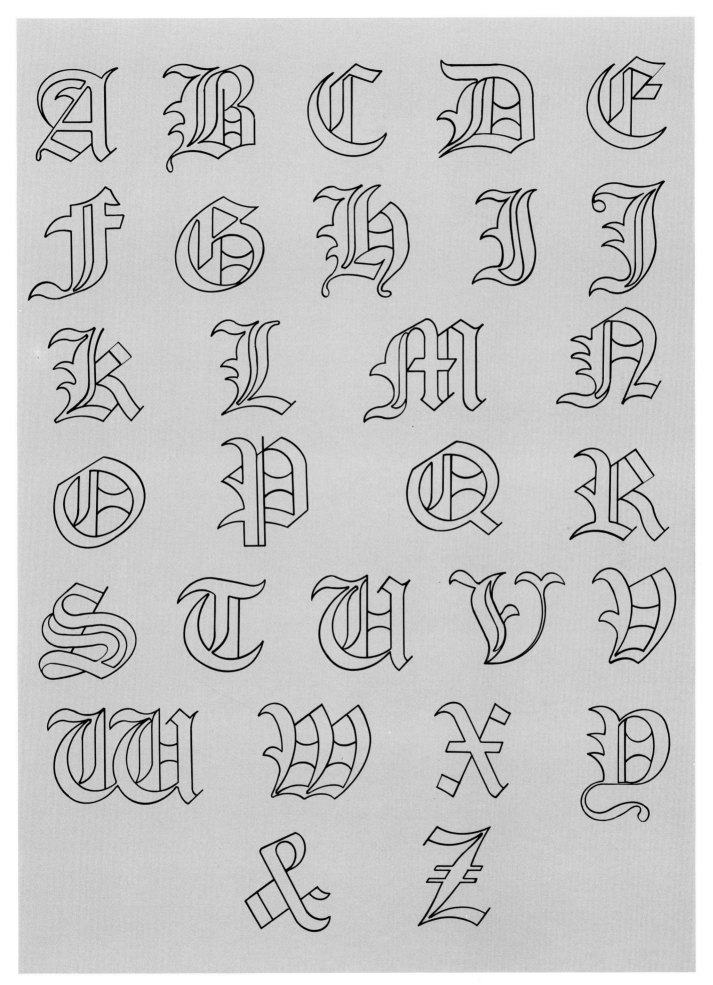

SIMPLE CHRISTMAS CAKE (p. 118)

STAR CAKE (p. 124)

*actual size*\*

SIMPLE CHRISTMAS CAKE (p. 118)

STAR CAKE (p. 124)

# INDEX

# LIST OF SUPPLIERS

**Retail and Mail Order**
The Country Store
2255 CR 27
Watterloo, In 46793
(219) 837-7440

Vern's Shoppe
2113 West Northern
Pueblo, Co 81001
(303) 564-6013

**Wholesale, Retail and Mail Order**
Parrish's Cake Decorating Supplies
314 West 58th Street
Los Angeles, Ca 90037-0368
(213) 750-7650

All About Cakes
11510 Woodside Avenue
Santee, Ca 92071
(619) 449-3643

Maid of Scandinavia
3244 Raleigh Avenue
Minneapolis, Mn 55416
(612) 925-9556

Wilton Enterprises, Inc
2240 West 75th Street
Woodridge, Ill 60517
(312) 963-7100

**Wholesale only**
The Country Kitchen
310 Racquet Drive
Fort Wayne, In 46825
(219) 484-2517

# CREDITS

The following cakes were designed
and demonstrated by Crumbs of
London: Mother's Day Cake (p. 128),
Thanksgiving Cornucopia (p. 134), Teddy
Bear's Picnic (p. 176), Water Lily
and Dragonfly (p. 178), Noah's Ark
(p. 180), Custom Car (p. 182),
Juke-Box (p. 184), Skier (p. 186),
Peacock (p. 188), Space Ship
(p. 190).
All the other cakes in the book
were designed and demonstrated by
Woodnutt's of Hove, Sussex.

Quarto would like to thank the
following for their assistance in
the preparation of this book:
G. T. Culpitt Limited, Hatfield, and the
Reject Shop, Beauchamp Place,
London.